LUCIFER
LEADERS

THE HIDDEN COST OF DEVIANT
BEHAVIOR IN THE SALES FORCE

PRAISE FOR LUCIFER LEADERS

"Kathy is the best at understanding the psychology of sales professionals and knows how to identify great sales professionals and provide world-class sales training. This book provides invaluable tips in these areas. What I love is Kathy is a great story teller, and not only is the book filled with knowledge, but the book is very funny and entertaining. Anyone who has worked with sales professionals, and specifically been a part of sales training classes, will be entertained from start to finish while obtaining great practical tips on hiring and training sales professionals!"

Tony Petrucci

Academic Director of Leadership Development, Temple University; President of DevelapMe: "The Real-time Feedback App"

"Lucifer Leaders will shatter every pre-conceived notion you have about salespeople — in the best possible way! With cleverest wit and humorous tone, Kathy Koultourides distills a gaggle of evil seller persona down to a practical and digestible mix of dos and don'ts for sales leaders, trainers, and human capital staff. *Spoiler Alert*: The most gregarious extrovert at the party is NOT your best seller, nor remotely close to your clients' zealous advocate. Invest in this pragmatic collection of war stories from a consummate master sales trainer, and save yourself from the nefarious sales demons lurking in your candidate pool!"

Alicia Shevetone

Sales Enablement Executive

"It's been more than a decade since Stanford professor Robert I. Sutton won the 2007 Quill Award for best business book with *The No Asshole Rule: Building a Civilized Workplace and Surviving One That Isn't*. The recent near-collapse of Wells Fargo due to its deviant sales culture indicates that the professor's ideas have gone unheeded or were not accompanied by practical means of implementation. With *Lucifer Leaders: The Hidden Cost of Deviant Behavior in the Sales Force*, Kathy Koultourides has written a long-needed book that not only exposes the significance of the problem, but clearly details how HR, sales managers and sales trainers can implement preventive and remedial solutions that readers can take back to the office. Kathy stunningly reveals why many sales-driven companies with the best of intentions are still recruiting the wrong candidates, like sunbathers unwittingly exposing themselves to the cancer-inducing radiation of sunlight. And that alone makes her book a must-read!"

Dan Coben
Executive Coach and Career Management Consultant

"If it is true that culture is based on whatever behaviors your organization will tolerate, *Lucifer Leaders* brings this point into clear focus. Scandal after scandal, Kathy Koultourides zooms in on sales people and sales leaders who have gone astray. She also offers a wide-angle view of how these behaviors can impact your company's culture and reputation. We may wish these stories were remnants of a bygone era, but we must be willing to acknowledge that no organization is immune to deviant and destructive forces from within."

Amy C. Waninger
Founder & CEO of Lead at Any Level LLC; Author of *Network Beyond Bias: Making Diversity a Competitive Advantage for Your Career*

"*Lucifer Leaders* will have a thought-changing impact on you and everyone responsible for the true cost to recruit, support, train and manage salespeople. Kathy Koultourides shares her keen insight and experiences that will challenge your thoughts from the past and guide those who can look through a fresh set of lenses. It will make a significant change in your perception and thought process toward what is a great salesperson. *Lucifer Leaders* will challenge your ideas of great traits and skills in a salesperson that can actually destroy a team with a financial impact of devastating proportions. This book is eye opening with a roller coaster ride of emotions to the point where I could not put it down. Kathy Koultourides takes us behind the scenes, sharing real stories with unexpected outcomes that could only be created by Lucifer Leaders."

Jim Holton
Sales Team Builder, Trainer and Culture Coach

"As I read *Lucifer Leaders*, I recalled many a training session with one or more "Lucifer" participants. I have over 20 years of Sales Training experience and have had one Lucifer, if not more, in each of my training sessions. Kathy Koultourides's book provided me with the types of "Lucifers" but more importantly how much those participants' deviant behaviors cost an organization. The breakdown of hidden cost was astounding and eye opening for me. This book has helped me identify the behaviors of each "Lucifer," and given me the confidence to provide feedback early in the onboarding process to their managers. I highly recommend this book to anyone who hires or manages a sales team. For those in the Training and Development field, *Lucifer Leaders* is a must-read book!"

Karen A. Connolly
Aramark, Regional Sales Trainer, Uniform Services

"How many times have you thought you were hiring the perfect sales reps only to find that you hired their evil twin? This is the message of *Lucifer Leaders* — a story of how hiring the wrong person (who looks perfect in the selection process) turns out to be the devil! Kathy Koultourides knows about Lucifer Leaders because she's worked with them and seen their evil ways first-hand. She tells a series of darkly funny (laugh-out-loud funny) true stories, and shares lessons learned. She also details the real costs for these bad hires. Everyone who hires, trains, or manages sales staff will want a copy of this book: to laugh, cry, and take heed of the lessons in it! Highly recommended!"

Cathy Fyock, SPHR, SHRM-SCP

"This is a must-read for all sales leaders trying to build a winning team! Kathy Koultourides has seen it all and shares true stories about the evils of Lucifer Sales Leaders and the high cost of hiring them. These people will harm your sales organization and cost your organization lots of money. Beware sales management professionals of your hiring practices. In her unique way, she will challenge you to think differently about how you hire and offers lessons for how to make improvements in your selection process. Grab a cup of coffee and enjoy the read. I guarantee you will be glad you did!"

Cathy Berlin
Sales Manager, Vogel Disposal Services, Inc.

"Kathy's ability to recount real-world examples of poor hiring practices will have more sales leaders and recruiters doubling down on their efforts to avoid the hidden and very tangible costs of making a bad hire. Kathy has lived in the crucible of the classroom with new hires. Like her, I know too well that feeling after the first day of a workshop. You retire to your room and ask yourself, 'Who the heck hired that guy?' In my work with selection assessments, nothing can trump the value and predictability of that training classroom. A fun must-read book, especially for frontline sales leaders."

John Hoskins
Author of *Level Five Selling*

"Kathy has taken her past experience across a multitude of businesses to show how easy it is to fall victim to outward appearances and superficial action if you do not delve into the details of a person's character. With clear and concise stories, *Lucifer Leaders* shows you how mistakes are made, the costs associated with those errors and, most importantly, how to correct the situation and put in processes to prevent the vicious cycle from repeating. Behavior matters."

Kevin Gaugush
Chief People Officer at Varsity Tutors

"We have all met or worked with this personality type. The appearance is very 'shiny' and appealing, and the team is instantly attracted to the glow. The damage that can be done by a Lucifer Leader is devastating and can be permanent if not recognized. Kathy's book gives us tools to identify this hiding charming 'demon' and teaches us how to avoid bringing them in to the fold in the first place. She does this with a book that is full of engaging stories that make it hard to put down. I recommend this book to other sales leaders and anyone who hires rain makers."

Maureen Solomon
Senior Sales Leader, MBA

"If you only invest in one business book this year, make it this one. Every business leader I know says hiring and retaining the right sales talent is, by far, their biggest challenge. Kathy Koultourides has cracked the code and offers us her time-tested roadmap from many decades of successful hiring, onboarding and training in the corporate world. Her remarkable track record for teaching others how to hire, onboard and train the right people speaks for itself — and it's all in this book. She outlines how to consistently make intelligent hiring decisions that serve the company and its customers for the long haul. Perhaps most importantly, she provides actionable steps to recognizing "a Lucifer" during the recruiting and interviewing process ... before investing in a bad hire. If there was a Hall of Fame for great hiring decisions, Kathy would be its first inductee."

Mike Monson
National Sales Manager of a Fortune 300 Company

"As an HR professional, I will be recommending this book to my colleagues and senior leadership! The real-life examples told in detail paint a clear picture of these Lucifer Leaders, and with wit and humor! Kathy's knowledge and experience shine through in educating the reader on how to evaluate, be on the lookout for, and deal with this breed of leader! I chuckled when Kathy explained how onboarding new employees gives such great insight, and she and her team became so good at predicting success. In the early part of my career, when conducting new hire orientation, I began to be able to pick the bad apples out in the first hour and eventually made it a game for myself with each new group, week after week, as to how long some of them would make it. Like Kathy, I became pretty accurate with my timing predictions. This book is a great, relatable and insightful read!"

Cassandra Yates
Chief Talent Officer, Performics US and Publicis Media Mexico

LUCIFER LEADERS

THE HIDDEN COST OF DEVIANT BEHAVIOR IN THE SALES FORCE

KATHY KOULTOURIDES

SILVER TREE
PUBLISHING

Pleased to meet you

Hope you guess my name

But what's puzzling you is the

Nature of my game.

Lyrics by Mick Jagger and Keith Richards
"Sympathy for The Devil."
Beggars Banquet. LP. Decca. 1968.

DEDICATION

To the BISCUITS Tin — A tiskit, a taskit. Oh the years they've been.
Remember funny stories with BISCUITS in a tin.

TABLE OF CONTENTS

CHAPTER ONE

The Backdrop

I spent 20 of my 34-year sales career in corporate training positions. I played the roles of sales training facilitator, designer and developer of sales training, manager, director, and executive of the sales training function. Throughout that time, it was the facilitation role that gave me true insight into what makes sales people tick. Over the years, I became highly sensitized to the behavior of sales professionals as a predictor of performance outcomes. My team and I got so good at seeing the future, for better or for worse, that we bested the top predictive indicator tools of the day. By the time I left my role as master sales training facilitator, we had an .875 batting average on who would be terminated within the next three months, and who should be terminated immediately.

How did we become so accurate in our predictions? It was because we spent a lot of time with the new hires. I mean a *lot* of time. We spent way more time with them than their own sales manager. Within the span of one week, we had more predictive intel than the average sales manager had spending the first three months with them. *How can that be,* you wonder? It stands to reason: they were a captive audience. We were present with them for breakfast, lunch, dinner, and then some, for days and sometimes weeks straight.

One of the reasons why the sales manager can't spend the time needed with the new hire stems from the assimilation process. A lot of companies have awkward onboarding and training practices that prevent them from getting a good look at who they've hired before it's too late. In some cases, the new hire is working remotely and unsupervised from the get-go. Some companies hire in cohorts and send them immediately to an immersion training session that can last anywhere from a few days to several weeks, thwarting any opportunity to "check under the hood" before making the commitment to spend the money on travel for training. Some companies provide initial onboarding at the local level to ready them for their job, spending anywhere from 30, 60, to 90 days, and then send the new hire to "sales training" to polish their skills around the company's methods, product knowledge, sales tools and processes. I'm a proponent of this practice because it gives the hiring manager time to assess and assimilate the new hire. Unfortunately, the manager doesn't always spend the amount of time needed in the crucial period just after hire. They often forego a proper onboarding and evaluation period, and stick the new hire smack-dab into the job in the first crucial week, overlooking behaviors that could provide clues to potential counterproductive workplace behavior.

> **Managers are often understaffed, as a result, they take short-cuts during the onboarding and evaluation period, overlooking behaviors that could provide clues to counterproductive workplace behavior.**

Over the years, I acquired experience with specific behaviors that, in hindsight, provided telltale signs of an unfit hire. On the surface, these sales professionals are everything that sales management and human resources are hoping for. They are driven and results oriented, and they can turn a perfect stranger into a "Best Friend Forever" in a matter of one conversation. They are hunters and they are closers. They score low on the conscientious and agreeability scale and high on the extroversion scale. Not only do they bend the rules, they break them. They are all of this, and over the top.

THE LUCIFER LEADER

This book shines a light on that certain type of salesperson that I call "The Lucifer Leader," an individual who has the capability to derail an organization by inciting other salespeople on the team to also engage in illicit activity. They do so to acquire power and position among their peers. As you learn about these "leaders," you will recognize many personality traits and behavior disorders that have crossed your career path over time. Throughout the book, I use real workplace stories to build a case for the elements that can identify this threat so that they can be eliminated from the organization, or never hired in the first place.

You will meet Charismatic Lucifer, who is the poster child for the Lucifer Leader. As you read the story, you will be shocked at the total cost of his influence. You will learn about Swindler Lucifer, who is a con artist in disguise and is a reminder to manage your hiring process effectively. You will meet Criminal Lucifer who can potentially ruin your brand, causing a disastrous public relations nightmare, but will learn what you can do to eliminate this risk. There is a chapter on Libertine Lucifer and how their attention-seeking behavior can rob you blind. You will learn about Monte Christo

Lucifer and how their wily ways can tank several sales teams at one time. You will learn about Voyeur Lucifer, a story beholden by competitiveness and the ultimate nightmare in the era of the #MeToo movement. You will meet Imperious Lucifer and see how the assumption of power and arrogance can cost you way more than you bargained for. Finally, you will meet Wardrobing Lucifer, whose behavior on the surface seems innocuous, but in reality, is a crystal ball into future behavior and performance.

ARE YOU READY TO MEET SOME LUCIFERS?

This book was written for sales managers and senior leaders, human resources professionals, sales trainers, business owners, and anyone touching the sales new hire in the recruiting, hiring, onboarding and training process.

If you are a sales manager, senior leader, or business owner you will learn the true costs associated with a bad hire, one who can derail your entire team, your business, and potentially your career. You will also learn what to look out for and the questions you need to ask to gain a deeper understanding about the "product" you are about to hire.

If you are a human resource professional, you will gain insight into the procedures that you can implement to mitigate the enormous costs that plague the sales force when a Lucifer Leader walks among you. You will also learn some strategies to help you to assist your constituents in the recruiting and hiring process.

If you are a sales trainer, you will learn to recognize the behaviors, the talk and the attitudes that Lucifer Leaders have up their sleeves. With your keen eye, you can help your sales managers diminish the blow they will feel at the hand of the Lucifer Leader.

While I'm not an academic, or a seasoned researcher who filled the pages of this book with graphs and charts of correlations to standard deviations, I do have more than 20 years of practical field experience. I've trained more than 4,000 sales reps in my day. I've seen it all. The good, the bad and the ugly, and I have a way of bringing out lessons learned through good story telling.

Why did you buy this book? It's simple. In today's mega-social media broadcast society of bad behavior, this book will help keep you out of the headlines. So, grab a cup of coffee and read through the stories. I guarantee you will learn something that you did not know and enjoy a chuckle or two along the way.

CHAPTER TWO

Charismatic Lucifer

They were all fired. All but one. Eleven sales people in total. In one fell swoop, they were gone. By my best estimation, we just lost nearly $1 million in sales force investment. This never happens, nor should it ever happen, until now. Sales Training Academy #24.

This was my first introduction to the Lucifer Leader. I had not recognized this type of leader behavior prior to the events that took place during this two-week training session. I call this leader the Charismatic Lucifer, and not in the positive inspirational sense, but in the compelling attraction that can influence the darker side of motivation sense. He is a convincing figure who uses his charm to manipulate the emotional reactions of others. He can bend the most sensible rationale into a perverted action. This is the story of Charismatic Lucifer (and the haunted conference center).

> The Charismatic Lucifer is a convincing figure who uses his charm to manipulate the emotional reactions of others. He can bend the most sensible rationale into a perverted action.

I was told that the Sugar Point conference center was haunted. No surprise, considering that the first building erected on the site was built in the late 1800's. Per the conference center brochure, Victorcliff as it is named, is a Victorian Mansion restored to its original magic and updated with modern amenities to provide meeting space and banquet-style dining for business meetings, conferences and training.

The property is very beautiful. It is settled on thirty-two acres of rolling tree-lined hills, with sweeping lawns and stunning panoramic views of the valley. It was named Sugar Point by the settlers who saw the land formation in the winter as a snow-capped mound of sugar. It looked like it would be a perfect location for our two-week Sales Training Academy. The Sales Training Academy is used to train new hires, with whom I refer to as "BISCUITS," who have already completed their four-week onboarding program and have been in the field actively selling for two to three months.

"BISCUITS" is a mnemonic that my training team made up: it stands for Business Internal Support Center United in Training Sales. Somewhere along the way, one of my training team members coined the phrase "BISCUITS Training" as an internal reference for our sessions. We did not publicly call it that; it was our internal moniker. Eventually the term BISCUITS became an endearing reference to the sales trainees. They came to us as raw dough, pliable and ready to rise. After we baked them for a week or so in our sales training program, they came out as fresh BISCUITS ready to entice any and all prospects into taking a bite.

I signed the contract to host my next Sales Training Academy ("Academy #24") and began the yeoman's work of a training facilitator. There were participant rosters to assemble, session memos to be sent to participants, subject matter expert facilitators to be confirmed, and materials to be gathered, sorted, boxed and transported. Sounds simple, but there are a lot of details, including attending to diva attendees who need special *everything*.

I was looking forward to this session because I really liked the facility. The food was outstanding, the meeting rooms were nice and big with comfortable ergonomic chairs, and large windows that provided natural light. The entire conference center was self-contained with running trails, fitness trails, swimming, tennis, game rooms, a BBQ and a fitness and rec center, tavern and dining options. Perfect! I wouldn't need to worry about transportation for off-site meals and entertainment for the participants during the entire two-week event.

Because my house was 43 miles away, I decided to stay at the conference center for the duration of the Academy. So, on Sunday I packed up my car and headed to Sugar Point to get everything set up for our Monday morning start. Upon arrival, I left the bulk of the materials in my car, grabbed my suitcase and checked in at the lodging center. I was handed the key for sleeping room #113. Like most conference centers, you need a trail of breadcrumbs to find your way back from wherever you came. After winding through several corridors, over an enclosed foot bridge, and down an elevator (yeah, I said *down*, totally confusing), I arrived at room #113.

I entered the room with a sigh of "meh." It seemed a little industrial. Cinderblock walls painted a color somewhere between pink, mauve and beige. It had two queen beds, and between the two beds was a night stand. Directly over the night stand was a coffee pot built into the cinderblock wall. Seemed a bit odd, but what the hell.

I threw my bag onto one of the beds and started to unpack. I hung up my clothes first, then headed into the bathroom to put away my toiletries. There really wasn't any room to put anything in the bathroom. It was super small. It had a ceramic free-standing sink with no countertop or cabinetry. There was a mirror over the sink, which I'm guessing was approximately 17 inches or so. There was a commode, and a shower with the same thematic color on the ceramic tiles as were on the cinderblock walls. There was one small metal shelf above the sink. It was maybe six inches deep and perhaps eighteen inches wide. Not much room for anything.

The only thing that really fit on the little metal shelf in the bathroom was the soap and the mini bottles of lotion, mouthwash and shampoo that the conference center provided each guest in a cute little basket. I took the first item out of the basket and set it on the metal shelf. No sooner than I was able to grab the second item, the first item leapt up off the shelf and slammed hard on the floor. It was almost as if someone had picked up the container and threw it to the ground with physical force. I didn't think too much about it. I picked up the container and placed it back on the shelf; again, the container mysteriously leapt from the shelf and was driven into the epoxy-coated concrete flooring. Now that got my attention! It was at this point when I remembered the conference center sales person joking with me that the place was haunted.

Being the somewhat superstitious person who I am, I picked up the container and looked around the room and said, "I apologize for intruding on your space, but I can't leave. I am going to be here for two weeks. I'm a nice person and I'm willing to respect your space if you can do the same for me. Perhaps we will both learn to get along with each other." I then placed the container on the shelf and it never moved again.

I realize that this sounds like a tall tale, but believe me, it is absolutely true! I saw the container slam to the floor, twice. There was no wind, no fan or air conditioner kicking on. There was no other way to explain it other than some strange supernatural poltergeist. I went about my business, tidying up before heading back to the car to get the classroom set up.

Meals at the conference center were held in the general dining room. Each company attending had tables with their company name on a metal stand in the middle of the table. It was about seven o'clock by the time I got to the dining room. By then, there were a few BISCUITS who had already checked-in and were having dinner. I made my way to their table and introduced myself, broke bread with them and learned a little bit about them.

There was Bethany, a new seller from the Wisconsin. She was very social and had good relating skills. She was polite and engaging. Seated next to her was Paul, a seller from Minnesota. Although Bethany and Paul did not know one another prior to this, they became acquainted quickly since both came from the Upper Midwest. Next to Paul was Kevin, who was quiet and seemed a bit shy. He was from an office that changed sales managers within the last three months since he was hired. Kevin sold printers before joining the company. After dinner, I walked them over to the meeting room to show them where it was and to help them feel more comfortable and acquainted with the space. Everyone was nice and polite, and it seemed like a good group. I said "goodnight" and returned to my room to retire for the evening.

No sooner did I fall asleep than the coffeemaker in the wall space turned on. It woke me up. As a facilitator of a lengthy program, the last thing one needs is a lack of sleep due to midnight interruptions. I heard this thing and thought, "What the hell? Is that the coffee maker?" I turned on the light and, sure enough, the coffee pot had kicked on and was making weird gurgling noises. The little brew light was glowing steady orange. I reached over and turned it off. This was not a coffee maker with a timer. It had one on/off switch. I definitely did not turn it on. I was sleeping! How did it turn on? Was it an electrical glitch?

Perhaps it was my invisible roommate, unable to resist temptation to convince me that the hotel was, indeed, haunted. One thing is for sure, it wasn't my mind playing tricks on me. The coffee pot turned on, by itself, in the middle of the night. When my alarm went off in the morning, I had nearly forgotten about the coffeemaker until I caught a glimpse of it out of the corner of my eye. I shook my head and got ready for work.

As the session kicked-off, we made introductions. We went around the room and each rep introduced themselves with our traditional ice breaker check list: name, location, previous experience, and objective for the session. First up was Kimberly, a very attractive girl, mid-to-late 20's. She came from the copier sales industry. Very confident and competitive. Her objective for the class was to learn everything she could to return to her branch office and position herself at the top of the sales rankings. Next came Brad, a jovial, rotund, fun-loving individual whose objective was to learn best practices from the other sales people in attendance. Third in line was Rob. Rob presented himself as smart and clever. He dressed well, carried himself with swagger and had a silver tongue. His objective was to supplement his existing selling skills and learn some new techniques. On to David; he was a southern gentleman. He was a little older than the first three, maybe by ten years or so. He was very polite and well-spoken, and said he wanted to learn more product knowledge. I continued around the room, introducing those I met at dinner the night before, along with the rest of the "fated twelve." Everything seemed to be going along perfectly.

Day one was a success. Day two was a success. Day three was a success. Everything was going according to schedule. The visiting dignitaries from the corporate office were on time and communicated upbeat messaging. The subject matter expert topic presenters were engaging and brought product demos. The smile sheets reflected an appreciative and engaged group of participants. It was a fun, but long week. By Friday, we were half-way through the two-week Academy. We had a full day on the schedule for Saturday, with Sunday off for reflection and refueling before beginning week two.

I had been running this Sales Training Academy for more than three years. We held a two-week session every eight weeks or so. This cohort was session number twenty-four (our soon-to-be the ill-fated "Academy #24"). All the reviews by participants past and present were stellar. We had a high percentage of successful outcomes from previous attendees. I had no reason to believe that this class would be any different. Until Saturday came around.

> **All the reviews by participants past and present were stellar. We had a high percentage of successful outcomes from previous attendees. I had no reason to believe that this class would be any different. Until Saturday came around.**

I slept well on Friday night, and in fact, I'll call it one of the best night's sleep of my facilitating career. I woke up refreshed and very upbeat. Perhaps I slept so well because of the exhausting efforts required to be a facilitator, event manager, guest speaker coordinator, and just plain old being "on" all day, every day for the past five days. Finally, Saturday had arrived. "Once I finish today's session, I will go home to spend Saturday night and part of Sunday at home before returning for week two," I thought.

With briefcase in tow, I headed toward the meeting room. As
I approached the enclosed foot bridge, one of the attendees stopped
me with a very disturbed look on his face. I said, "Good morning,"
and he replied, "I don't think so, and I have never been so embarrassed to be part of a company."

Whoa. "What happened? What are you talking about?" I said.
"I don't even want to discuss it. It makes me sick. I am disgusted," he
replied. He went on, "If you want to know, I suggest you speak with
hotel security."

This is not what a facilitator wants to hear first thing in the morning.
So, I hauled myself down to the security office. When I walked in,
I saw the same dreaded look on the face of the head of security for the
conference center. "I just ran into one of my attendees in the hallway
and he was very upset about something that happened last night. He
wouldn't tell me what it was. In fact, he said he couldn't even talk
about it because it was so upsetting to him. Did something happen?"
I said to the security director.

"Come in to my office and have a seat," he said, as he picked up the
phone to call the Director of Sales for the Conference Center to join
us. This is the person with whom I signed the event contract. And
here was the conversation that ensued:

"There was a serious incident that happened last night, and it
involved several of your attendees," the security director said.
"What in the world happened?" I asked. "Here's what we know," he
responded. "In the early morning hours, around three a.m., a large
group of your attendees returned to the property from an outing.
They were intoxicated and were very loud. They began roaming the
halls of our facility. One person took a fire extinguisher from the wall
and started spraying it under guest room doors. They also discharged

the extinguisher into the ice machine. They were banging on guest room doors, waking up guests and causing a big disturbance," he said. The sales director chimed in, "We had several calls come in to the front desk. And, worse, our best, recurring customer told us that they will no longer do business with us. They book one three-day retreats every month for thirty people. That will be a huge revenue hit to the property!"

This is very disturbing. I am in complete disbelief. *My* people? I've been with them for five straight days, and I can't believe they would do this! "Are you sure it was my people?" I ask. "Yes, we have them on video surveillance. I'm surprised that you didn't hear anything. This happened on the same floor that you are on." My heart is in my throat. I feel my face go flush. I asked, "What is your next step?" The security director responded, "We will complete a full investigation, and determine our course of action when the investigation concludes."

Naturally, I was mortified. I apologized up and down and let both directors know that I was taking this very seriously and would involve our corporate management team immediately. This was bad, very bad. I was embarrassed for my company, its reputation, and for the fact that something like this could have happened on my watch. I headed down to the meeting room and began setting up.

> **This was bad, very bad. I was embarrassed for my company, its reputation, and for the fact that something like this could have happened on my watch.**

As the clock got closer to 8:00 a.m., the attendees began to trickle in. The room was set up in a U-shape configuration, with the attendees in the U and my seat at a table at the front, facing them. I continued to organize my materials. The room was silent. There wasn't the usual chit-chat that usually happens before the beginning of class.

When everyone was seated, I finished organizing my flip charts and sat down at my seat in the front. I surveyed the room in silence, making purposeful eye contact with each participant in the U. I opened with, "Who wants to tell me what happened last night?" Dead silence. Not one person spoke up. I sat quietly for a couple of minutes, continuing to scan the group eyeball to eyeball. I asked again. And again, I heard only crickets. "We are not going to start until I hear what happened, even if it takes all day." It's hard to believe that 12 people would sit in silence. Even the guy I spoke to in the hallway on my way to the session, the one who was disgusted, didn't speak up.

I continued to sit in silence, looking at each of their faces. Their puffy faces. Their red eyes. All evidence of too much alcohol and not enough sleep. I began asking pointed closed-ended questions to specific people. Slowly they started talking, but most of what they were feeding me were lies. "So and so broke his toe while we were at the dance club and we had to help him back to his room, and we accidentally ran into a couple of hotel room doors." Blah, blah, blah.

Finally, about thirty minutes into this, I saw a police car driving slowly up the long, winding drive. I could see the car as the windows were facing me. Perfect. "Well, the police are finally here. I'm sure that they will be reviewing the surveillance video. We will get down to the bottom of this shortly," I said.

Simultaneously, like 12 kittens following a feather on a string, they turned around to look out the window. Their heads snapped back to a forward position so fast that you'd think I had fired a gun in the air. Suddenly, the confessions started pouring out. A majority went to a bar. They got really drunk. They were kicked out of the bar. They had to find their way back to the conference center. Someone broke a toe, someone threw up, someone grabbed the fire extinguisher, and then another, and then another, with each person trying to outdo the other with a better stupid stunt. I took a lot of notes.

In fact, I could not write nearly as fast as they were dishing on one another. After they got everything out on the table, I told them to wait in the classroom while I met with security. I walked down to the security office and had a conversation with the director. It turned out that the police car was just a coincidence. The cops weren't there to investigate this incident.

The hotel was willing to give me some time to speak with my higher-ups. So, I headed back to the classroom. I was half-shocked to see that they were all still in the room sitting in their seats. "This is a very serious situation and a very bad reflection on our company," I said. "As the manager of this Academy, I am required to file a serious incident report with our legal team and inform our senior leaders. I am shutting this session down, effective immediately, and advise each of you to remain in your rooms until Monday morning when you will learn the consequences of your actions."

They were all scared, and they felt bad, physically and emotionally. I left the facility, giving my personal contact information to the front desk and security director with instructions to call me immediately if they heard one peep out of them. My next call was to my boss, and to our General Counsel. Those were tough calls. It happened on my watch; I am the leader. How could I have let this happen? Was it my fault? How in the world did I sleep through all the racket? I'm a light sleeper. I would and should have woken up. To this day, I still wonder if it was the poltergeist ensuring that I heard nothing, allowing the melee to ensue, and enjoying the action as if it were the instigator who was finding peace in the burden that I must now carry forward.

> **My next call was to my boss, and to our General Counsel. Those were tough calls. It happened on my watch; I am the leader. How could I have let this happen? Was it my fault?**

By the end of Saturday, I spoke with both my boss and our General Counsel. We decided to send everyone home on Monday, which meant that I would need to facilitate the discharge. I involved our corporate travel department to change everyone's flights, contacted the attendees' managers and let everyone know the steps in the investigation from the company's end. On top of that, I assuaged the hotel and apologized up and down, promising that we would fulfill our contractual obligation even though we were leaving a week early. And, I apologized in person to their "number-one" client.

In the end, we fired all but one of the 12 participants. We paid for the fulfillment of our contract as if we ate, slept and continued our training for the balance of the following week. I was able to get the conference center's number-one customer to accept our apology and not hold it against the hotel. They continued to book their monthly events without incident, allowing the hotel to continue to capture the revenue they forecasted from this client.

If I were reading this story, I'd be dying to know the results from the company's internal investigation, which, by the way, cost the company $36,000 (and this is the cost for *just the internal investigation*). I will share it with you now: Let's start with Rob. The team looked up to him; he was polished and self-confident with a quick wit and silver tongue. The group was attracted to his lone wolf style. He ran his book of business *his* way, not necessarily by the book, or by the principles set up by the organization. Throughout the week, he often opined of his sales conquests, citing examples of his techniques which weren't exactly conventional, or by the prescription taught in the sales training. His renegade attitude captured the enchantment of the others.

> The team looked up to Rob; he was polished and self-confident
> with a quick wit and silver tongue. The group was attracted
> to his lone wolf style.

Rob convinced everyone that they deserved a night out on the town because of the hard work they put in to the workshop the past week. He cozied up to Kimberly during the week and added that "dancing" should be part of the celebration. Rob directed Brad, the jovial one, to secure transportation for the group. They picked a popular club where all the best-in-class singles go to party.

Rob led the group through the red velvet ropes that formed a pathway directly to the bouncer. It was $15 per person to get in the door. Rob used his skills to secure a volume discount for the group of 11. They pooled their money together and entered the first lobby bar. It was dark with strobe lights gyrating to the beat of the music from the disc jockey's turntables. The group scattered about the club, eventually finding themselves on the dance floor. Later they took a break from the sardine can and headed to their appointed booth. That was when Rob inspired the group to do shots. The first round was "Sex-On-The-Beach" and it was so good that they had to have another round, and a third, before half of them headed back to the dance floor.

This gave Rob a chance to manage Kevin. Kevin was the introvert. This type of club was way over his head, so Rob took it upon himself to lead Kevin to a new life of excitement. He baited him to connect with a girl who was seated at a table by herself, tapping on her phone.

He even generated some opening lines that might work well for Kevin. They settled on a ploy whereby Kevin would greet the girl with a request for help with his non-functioning phone, which happened to be the same kind she was holding. Kevin got up his nerve, and within 30 seconds he took a seat with Miss Lonesome.

On their next break, Rob ordered a bottle of champagne for Kimberly. All the pretty girls in the club had a bottle of champagne at their tables, the bubbly glasses perched in their hands like expensive accoutrements. They sipped and giggled as the effervescence framed their faces with sparkles. Kimberly felt like a queen, a complete part of the experience. They don't have these types of clubs in the small Midwest city where she is from.

The dance floor was crowded, in fact, packed. It looked like one giant mass of humanity bobbing and weaving to the rhythm of the colored strobes. Rob grabbed Kimberly by the hand and they weaved and bobbed their way to the middle of the dance floor. They danced close, Rob holding Kimberly up on her high heels so that she wouldn't get swallowed up by the crowd. They got closer and closer and made their way off the dance floor stuck together like glue.

Kimberly slid into the booth, grabbing the bottle of champagne and taking a swig straight from the bottle. By the time the bottle was turned upside down in the side bar, Kimberly was face down in Rob's lap.

Brad came back off the dance floor and slid into the booth next to them. He took one look at Kimberly and asked Rob if she was passed-out. Rob was in a trance. Brad downed the rest of his beer and headed back out to the dance floor. By this time, one of the bouncers realized what was going on in the booth, and hustled Rob and Kimberly promptly out of the club.

As they were being forcibly escorted from the club, Kevin took notice. He bolted from Miss Lonesome and followed in hot pursuit not knowing if Rob and Kimberly were ditching them or if something else was happening. Kevin shouted his name several times, but Rob would not turn around. Once they cleared the doors, Kevin caught up with them outside. Kimberly didn't look good. She was disheveled and needed physical assistance to stand upright. Rob looked at Kevin and told him that they kicked Kimberly out of the club because she was over-served, and that Rob came along to make sure that she would get back to the hotel safely.

Kevin asked Rob about the others; should he go back into the club and round everyone up so that they can leave together? Rob told Kevin to go back inside and have fun, and that the rest of the group could get a couple of taxis back to the conference center. Kevin was unsure of this course of action, but Rob looked like he had everything under control, so he turned around and went back inside to let the others know what was going on.

It was getting late, or should I say, early in the morning. So, while Rob and Kimberly started to make their way back to the conference center, Kevin rounded up the rest of the group and together they fumbled for transportation, trying to remember the name of the facility they needed to return to. Somehow, by the Grace of God, they got back to the hotel, but not without incident.

One of the cab drivers insisted that they did not pay their fare in full and threatened to call the cops if they didn't pay up. To avoid trouble, they worked out a deal where two of the guys would stay behind with the driver while the others went in to secure the funds. They had to find Rob, but could not remember which room he was in. They started pounding on doors randomly, laughing and carrying on like a bunch of drunken frat boys. As they turned the corner toward the next wing, they ran smack into Rob and Kimberly who were just now stumbling their way back. Rob gave them some money and they asked Kimberly if they could go into her purse and get the rest of what they needed, with a promise to pay her back. Kimberly mumbled something incoherently, which gave the boys the nod they needed to rifle through her purse.

With the taxi incident behind them, the group raucously stumbled back to the sleeping quarters of the conference center. As they approached the floor, they took notice of Kimberly crumpled up in a heap next to the ice machine; and this they thought was funny. Rob suggested she looked like something from *A Weekend at Bernie's*. That was all the impetus that Brad needed to grab the fire extinguisher off the wall and position it with Kimberly to give her the appearance of riding a mechanical bull with the hose as her rein. The extinguisher was heavy and as Brad repositioned it, it discharged. Brad recoiled and landed ass-over-end, crashing into a guestroom door directly across from the ice machine. Everyone roared. William could not resist grabbing the fire extinguisher and discharging it right where the sun doesn't shine on Brad's backside. And so, the melee began.

The group whipped themselves into a frenzy, spray-painting the walls with the fire extinguisher and discharging it under the guest room doors. As guests started phoning the front desk, Brad dropped the extinguisher on his foot, which injured his toe to the point where it was bleeding. He pulled off his shoe and stuck his foot in the ice machine. William grabbed the fire extinguisher, and with grand proclamation, announced that he would put out the fire; he promptly emptied the extinguisher into the ice machine on top of Brad's bleeding foot. With nothing left in the extinguisher, the group disbanded and retired to their respective rooms leaving their Lucifer signature behind.

TRAIT COMPETITIVENESS

Let's break this story down: Who was the Lucifer Leader? If you guessed Rob, you guessed right. The lone wolf. The swagger. The silver tongue. There was something about him that was of interest. He had an air of mystery fueled by his unorthodox tactics. It was his "don't play by the rules" approach that is most revealing. "Cavalier" screams lack of respect, and when you have lack of respect for process and the order of the organization, trouble usually follows. But more important to identifying this type of Lucifer Leader is this: he was the type of rep that many sales managers and HR managers love. He was self-confident, competitive, worked hard, played harder and played to win.

> **"Cavalier" screams lack of respect, and when you have lack of respect for process and the order of the organization, trouble usually follows.**

Sales people tend to be competitive. It's a characteristic that many hiring managers seek. In fact, it should be noted that this company's selection tool measured competitiveness as a key trait for employment consideration. Our Lucifer scored off-the-chart on the competitiveness scale.

Interestingly, some researchers question the pursuit of highly competitive salespeople. Kohn (1992) argues that competitiveness can drive employees to sabotage the efforts of people they should be helping because highly competitive individuals are, by their nature, more likely to view others as competitive threats.[1]

---

1   Alfie Kohn, *No Contest: The Case Against Competition* (Boston: Houghton Mifflin, 1986/1992).

In their research on the effect of trait competitiveness on salesperson deviance, Ronald Jelinek and Michael Ahearne explain how organizational fit discourages deviant salesperson behavior, and how trait competitiveness and long hours motivate various forms of deviance.[2] The result of their research brought to light "with surprising consistency" that hiring managers want sales people who were competitive and willing to work long hours. I don't think that anyone reading this would argue their finding. They go on to surmise that "the negative relationship between fit and deviance should be a strong reminder of the need for rigorous hiring and screening practices."

⇒ LUCIFER LESSON #1 ⇐
Applicant Screening

For the HR professional who assumes the role of applicant screener — Partner with your sales management constituents to truly understand the role you are recruiting and screening for. I was speaking with a seasoned sales trainer while writing this book, and she talked a lot about the level of talent that passes through her training sessions. It's been less-than-stellar and new hire turnover is high. When I asked what she thought the problem was, she mentioned that the folks in recruiting don't have a handle on the job of the sales rep or the cultural environment at the local level. That's some food for thought.

---

2   Ronald Jelinek and Michael Ahearne, "Be Careful What You Look For: The Effect of Trait Competitiveness and Long Hours on Salesperson Deviance and Whether Meaningfulness of Work Matters," *Journal of Marketing Theory and Practice* 18, no. 4 (Fall 2010): 303–321. 2010 M.E. Sharpe, Inc.

> **Partner with your sales management constituents to truly understand the role you are recruiting and screening for.**

I would recommend to HR recruiters and screeners to spend a day riding with a seasoned sales rep in the field. Develop a relationship with the sales managers that you serve. Review the screening questions that you use and make sure that they align with the role and the values of the company. Truly understand how the compensation works, the hours required, and the working conditions. Ask screening questions that uncover fit for the role and the environment the role operates in.

⫸ LUCIFER LESSON #2 ⫷
Organizational Fit

Make sure that organizational fit is weighted higher than trait competitiveness during the recruitment and selection process. Organizational fit provides the pathways to employee engagement and gives them a sense of control. In the case of our Lucifer here, his "lone wolf" bravado is a key indicator that he lacks organizational fit.

Let's examine this for a minute: How do you screen for organizational fit? Start with your company's guiding principles. Ask questions that align with your company's values. For example, one of the guiding principles at this company reads, "*We will always act in the best interest of our team, our organization and our customers.*" What value is this guiding principle driving at? Did you answer, "trust, cooperation, and respect"? Yes. Now let's think about the qualities of a person that would align with these values. We might look for someone who is committed to our vision, they treat others with consideration and courtesy, and they are accountable to the goals of the team.

> ## What kind of interview questions might help you identify a candidate who would make a good cultural fit?

What kind of interview questions might help you identify a candidate who would make a good cultural fit? First, make sure that you are asking a solid behavior-based question, not a hypothetical-type question. Behavior-based questions provide a spring-board for the candidate to answer by describing the context of the situation, the task that required the action they took, and the result of their action. A good behavior-based question that will help you understand the candidate's alignment with the company's culture of teamwork might sound like this: "Tell me about a time when you made a decision to work outside of the established principles of the organization. Why did you make that decision, and what was the result?" This is a much better approach than asking the question in a hypothetical way. Hypothetical questions start with, "What would you do if …" While some people may argue that this type of question will get at underlying personality traits, any candidate can project what they would do, which is entirely different than what they actually do. For a behavior-based interviewing guide visit www.luciferleaders.com.

⋙ LUCIFER LESSON #3 ⋘
Meaningfulness of Work

Make sure that the hiring manager or the HR rep or the trainer who is responsible for the orientation and onboarding process takes the time to share the meaningfulness of the work that the new hire will be doing. Studies show that by strongly communicating the meaningfulness of the work, as it relates to the overall welfare of the organization, will reduce the potential for deviant behavior. Make sure that they understand how they fit into the bigger picture, and how their work is important to the overall well-being of the team and the company. Reinforce the mission, vision, guiding principles and values. All too often this is reviewed during orientation, a.k.a. the first three days on the job. After that, the rest of the training on job duties are never really tied back to the all-important company values.

> **Find ways to make sure that your training continually reaches back to your company's core values.**

Think about it, do your job descriptions link to your organization's values? Does your training program continually link back to company values? Can your new hires recite the company mission and core values three months after they've been hired? Can they communicate it correctly to customers? To Friends? To Family? And, more important, to other new hires down the road? If your answer is no, find ways to make sure that your training continually reaches back to your company's core values. Some ways to do this might be during role-play evaluation. In addition to the core skills that are being practiced and observed, ask role-play observers to provide feedback on how the company values and principles were displayed during the role-play.

⋙ LUCIFER LESSON #4 ⋘
Training Hours

Reduce training hours to include more breaks and reflection. Sales people are not used to sitting in a seat all day long. They lose focus and become separated from the meaningfulness of the work they are doing during training workshops, and this can increase the potential for deviant behavior. What I've learned from the front lines of the classroom is that those long hours most likely always contribute to the potential for sales people to go overboard at the bar. They are cooped up for too long and when it's time to cut loose, they do it in the spirit of go big or go home. Think about it, what is the start and stop time for your typical training workshop?

In my experience, the company always wants to stuff too much information into the time they have budgeted for. Training workshops usually start at 8:00 a.m. and end at 5:00 p.m., with a 10 to 15-minute break in the morning, an hour for lunch and a 10 to 15-minute break in the afternoon. (Quite frankly, I feel that this is too long of a day for training to be effective). But, what usually happens is that there is too much material to cover, the lunch break gets condensed, the breaks are rushed, you run over by 30 minutes, and then there's homework for participants to complete in the evening. Yes, it is the training facilitator's job to keep the training on track, but no matter how hard we try, we are often given direction to add content or allow time for "visiting dignitaries" who use up too much air. Before you know it, we have turned 7 ½ hours of "butts in seats" into 8 ½ hours. That's enough to drive anyone to drink!

My recommendation is to cut the seat time down, and *way down*. I want to start at 8:30 a.m. and end at 4:30 p.m. or start at 8:00 a.m.

and end at 4:00 p.m., or start at 8:00 a.m. and build in two 30-minute breaks and also honor the hour-long lunch break. Be sure to add enough time for proper debrief and reflection of key learning points. Give participants time to digest and process key learnings before trying to push more into their brains.

> **Be sure to add enough time for proper debrief and reflection of key learning points. Give participants time to digest and process key learnings before trying to push more into their brains.**

➤ LUCIFER LESSON #5 ➤
Organizational Citizenship

Reward good organizational citizenship behavior and penalize poor organizational citizenship behavior. Organizational citizenship, as defined by *BusinessDictionary.com,* is: "The extent to which an individual's voluntary support and behavior contributes to the organization's success."[3] By establishing strong values and reinforcing the importance of those values, you will help develop good organizational citizenship. To do this, you need to establish what the expectations are and the consequences of stepping over the boundaries. Recently, I had a conversation with a director of organizational development at a large global conglomerate. She told me that her company established a zero tolerance policy for the entire sales organization. If anyone crosses or steps outside the guardrails, they are fired, no matter how high they rank on the sales leader

---

3   Read more: http://www.businessdictionary.com/definition/organizational-citizenship.html.

board. She went on to tell me how tough it is for sales managers to take out the axe, especially when it falls squarely on the head of the "uber producer."

> **By establishing strong values and reinforcing the importance of those values, you will help develop good organizational citizenship.**

Another interesting component of this story is how so many people in the cohort who collaborated in the poor behavior would not rat each other out — even the one individual who was most appalled at the behavior of his peers. As a sales manager or HR professional, how do you know that deviant behavior is happening before it's too late, especially if no one is willing to come forward and report?

According to an article in the *Journal of Military Psychology*, there are three factors that seem to influence peer reporting of counterproductive workplace behavior:[4]

The emotional closeness between the person exhibiting the "counter workplace behavior" and the person observing it. In this case, the Academy training participants were somewhat close. All the participants had been living with each other day and night for five straight days and were encamped in a remote location with little freedom outside the property.

---

4   *Situational Factors Affecting Peer Reporting Intentions at the U.S. Air Force Academy: A Scenario-Based Investigation*, Gordon J. Curphy, Frederick W. Gibson, Gary Macomber, Callie J. Calhoun, Leigh A. Wilbanks & Matthew J. Burger Pages 27-43 | Published online: 17 Nov 2009.

The severity of the misconduct observed and the presence of witness(es). While the misconduct was severe, to the participants these were viewed as "goof-off" pranks.

Peers are more likely to report the counter workplace behavior (CWB) of colleagues when the conduct is severe, or when there are other witness(es) present. They are less likely to report the conduct when they are emotionally close to the person or people committing the CWB. In this case, the confessions started pouring out when the group learned that there was surveillance video and law enforcement was on its way to review the "electronic" witness! This turned their "goof-ball" pranks into severe misconduct with equally severe potential consequences.

Trainers and managers take note: When you make the work of the sales person meaningful, in both the context of training and the context of the job, you are providing a pathway to motivation and personal development. These pathways lead to empowerment. The more empowered your sales force is, the less likely they are to be provoked by the nature of their inherent competitiveness and the long hours they must spend on the job as well as in training.

HIDDEN COSTS FROM THE CHARISMATIC LUCIFER

What are the hidden costs in this story? Let's walk through the fundamentals: We fired 11 sales people, each with a salary of $55,000. The "ill-fated 11" were on the payroll for a total of 13 weeks prior, costing the company $151,250 in lost base salary. Add to that the benefits costs of $17,490 (healthcare, car allowance, disability and life insurance), and that brings the cost to $168,740. These are the only surface

costs, representing just the wages paid during their 90-day orientation and onboarding period.

Let's dive a little deeper into the hard costs. Consider the pre-hire
costs: application processing, interviewing, pre-hire assessment
costs, drug screening, background check, and agency fees. All tolled,
the sum-total per hire just for these expenses is $820 x 11 = $9,020.
We're up to $177,760. Now we need to add the training costs which
includes travel, transportation, housing, food and beverage, plus
materials and supplies totaling $28,241 — and let's not forget to
add to that the cost to discharge everyone early, which includes
re-booking change fees, corporate travel agent time, conference
center penalties for breach of contract at a cost of $24,200. We're
up to $230,201. That's nearly a quarter of a million dollars just for
hard costs!

If you think that's it, no way. Now, for the *real* hidden dollars, the soft
costs. The costs that you don't consider. These are the BIG, HUGE
costs: Lost opportunity (vacancy cost), replacement cost, low morale
cost and lost customer cost!

Let's start with lost opportunity cost. If these 11 sales people
performed at the level of others who graduated from the Sales
Academy, the company would have realized $250,000 quota revenue,
per person, multiplied by 11, equaling $2,750.000. Our cost for this
loss just jumped to $2,773,201.

Consider this: The terminations have left territories vacant,
causing account management to suffer and ultimately resulting
in lost customers. Don't think for one minute that our competitors won't jump on the chance to steal our customers when there
is even a sniff of poor service, or that no one is paying attention to
the customer. Just one customer breach has consequences. A single

three-year contract loss can cost the company $18,000 in annual revenue ($18,000 x 11 = $198,000). And what about the sales people who remain on the team? They must pick up the slack for the terminated reps. They must work longer hours and establish relationships with customers that they don't know well; they're overworked, their productivity can decline and their morale can drop to a level that might very well cost the company more voluntary turnovers.

If this isn't bad enough, there is the cost of replacement for the terminated employees *and* for the one you didn't anticipate replacing.

By now your head should be spinning. So, what did this Lucifer cost the company? Wait for it ... $2,971,201. And to think that I originally estimated $1 million. Ha! I was only $2 million off base. That's a huge hidden cost!

As for the sole survivor? It was David, the guy who ran into me on the foot bridge that fateful Saturday. He went on to become a fine sales person.

On the following page is a great Cost of Turnover Worksheet that was created by Cara Silletto from Crescendo Strategies. I'm sharing it with her permission. It's a good guideline to get you started!

Cost of Turnover Worksheet

Complete this form separately for each type of position.

Position: _____ Hrly Rate: _____ Times Filled Per Year: _____

PER HIRE COSTS

Direct Labor Costs: _____

- Application Processing
- Interview
- Analysis & Selection

Hiring Costs: _____

- Drug Screening
- Background Check
- Agency Fees
- Other (Relocation, etc.)

Wages during Orientation: _____

- Direct Compensation
- Indirect Compensation

Support Staff Costs (Per Hire): _____

- Accounting Time
- HR/Benefits Time

Supply Costs (Per Hire): _____

- Safety Equipment
- Uniforms
- Other Supplies (Business Cards, Vehicle, etc.)

Lost Productivity (Per Hire): _____

- Identify Days to Full Productivity
- Calculate as # * hrly rate * 50% * 8 hrs/day

OTHER COSTS

Training Costs (Annual): _____

- General Orientation Time
- Specific Job Training Time
- Training Materials
- Calculate * # Groups Trained/Year

Overtime Costs (Annual): _____

- Due to short staffing

Recruiting Costs (Annual): _____

- Generic or Targeted Ads
- Other (Job Fairs, etc.)

ANNUAL COST CALCULATIONS

Per Hire Total Costs: _____

x

Number Hired Per Year: _____

=

_____

+

Other Costs (Annual Total): _____

=

TOTAL ANNUAL COSTS _____

Note: This is Per Position in Organization.

Contact Cara Silletto at cara@crescendostrategies.com for help reducing employee turnover. © 2016 Crescendo Strategies

Used with permission from Cara Silletto at Crescendo Strategies

CHAPTER THREE

Swindler Lucifer

Lucifer Leaders sneak up on you when you least expect it. Sometimes, it's the one who appears most vulnerable and slightly disadvantaged. You don't realize it because it is in your human nature to try and lift this person, lending a helping hand to one who has worked hard to reach his/her current level of success. This type of Lucifer sucks the kindest and most genuine people into its snare. They garner trust through a simple and convenient exposure to their life of disadvantage. They are the underdog. People like to rally around the underdog. They become inspired by their challenges and with utopic humanitarian gestures, and they unwittingly help this Lucifer lead with unabashed resolve. This Lucifer cost the company a bundle — to the tune of more than $137,000. This is the story of Swindler Lucifer.

> The Swindler Lucifer sucks the kindest and most genuine people into its snare. They garner trust through a simple and convenient exposure to their life of disadvantage. They are the underdog.

It's always an ominous sign when a training attendee approaches the facilitator and asks if he can speak with you in private. It usually has nothing to do with the training.

He had a distressed look on his face, not quite panic, but a reserved, borderline look of panic. It was just the right amount of panic for a person who likes to maintain an even keel, as his personality dictates. This is the guy who spent his training "off hours" in Bermuda shorts and Hawaiian shirts. He was maybe mid-40's and quite personable. He brought many years of B2B sales experience to the company. I remember him particularly for his laid-back personality, but he also carried himself with an air of maturity.

He seemed hesitant about how to bring the subject up to me. As if he was embarrassed, or at the very least, wishing he did not need to have the conversation at all. Somehow, he got his nerve up, took a deep breath, and proceeded with his story:

> "Last night, I went down to the pool for some R&R. I must not have been paying attention because when I was getting ready to head back to my room, I noticed that my watch and wallet were missing. I looked everywhere and could not find them. Then, I thought that maybe I left them in my room, but I couldn't find the key either. I thought that maybe I lost the key in the pool, but it was too dark to see."

I asked, "Did you report it to hotel security?" "No," he said, and continued, "I just went to the front desk to get a replacement key and figured that I would find my watch and wallet in the room."

I could see that this might be embarrassing for this guy. He probably didn't want me to think that he was scatterbrained or something. But, I'm still waiting for the *ask* when he said, "When I got back to the room, my watch and wallet were nowhere to be found, so I'm going to need some petty cash and a new driver's license to get back home."

Boom! There it was: petty cash and a driver's license. As I took this in, my mind started to process. Well, it's only Wednesday, and I've got some time to help bridge the gap for this guy. I need to talk to Finance and see how we can get him some funds and talk to HR to figure out how to get a replacement identification for the trip home. Repeating myself, I asked, "Did you report this to hotel security?"

"No, not yet, I wanted to let you know first," he said.

Hmmm. That's a bit odd, but I am dealing with a person who is from out of state and new to the company. He probably doesn't want to rock the boat by going straight to hotel security. Or, maybe he feels more comfortable dealing with this through me? It's not unusual for a parent-child relationship to develop between training facilitator and trainee, a phenomenon that all highly-skilled facilitators can relate to. I can understand that.

"Let's head down to the security office right now and let them know about this," I said. We headed to the front desk. I'm no stranger to this property and quite frankly, I am considered a VIP for all the business that I throw their way. I know everyone at the front desk, and I know all the banquet and catering people, the entire sales staff, the executive staff, and of course, I know the security staff.

I walked straight past the front desk, greeting the staff on my way back to the business office with my attendee right at my heels. I peeked my head in to the security office, and thankfully, the director was at his desk. "Do you have a minute, Ron?" I asked. "Sure, what's up?" "This is Paul, one of my training attendees. Last night, he was at the pool and his watch and wallet came up missing. I'm thinking that he should probably file a report or something."

Ron replied, "Well, this isn't good. I'm very sorry to hear about this. It's nice to meet you, Paul. I'm sorry to hear about your missing belongings. Yes, we will need to fill out a report, give me a sec to get it." Ron brought out the necessary paperwork and asked Paul to have a seat. He proceeded to ask all the usual questions: name, address, phone number, room number, and his version of what happened.

Paul began, "I went down to the pool after dinner at around 8:00 pm. The weather was so nice, and I wanted to take advantage of the quiet time to review what we learned in class and prepare for today. I set my stuff down on the cocktail table next to my chaise lounge and started reading through my notes. The pool was like glass. No one was in the pool. My eyes just kept wandering from my notes to the pool, so I decided to take a dip. I jumped in and swam a couple of laps, and then I got out and toweled off." "Were there other people at the pool while you were there?" asked Ron. "Not initially, but when I got out of the pool, a couple of people came in and took a few chairs." "Did you know these people; did they look familiar; can you describe them?" Ron asked. "No, they didn't look familiar. They were seated all the way across the pool from me, and they were pretty engrossed in their own conversation, so I don't think they had anything to do with it," Paul said swiftly.

"Can you describe them to me?" Ron said. "No, not really, it was dark. It was a man and a woman. They had street clothes on and they were drinking cocktails." "Approximately what time was it when they came to the pool?" Ron asked. "Oh, I don't' know, maybe 45 minutes after I sat down." "And, when did you notice that your belongings were missing? It was a watch and wallet, correct?" "Yes, my watch and wallet. At first, I thought that maybe I left them in my room, and just *thought* that I set them down on the table. So, I gathered up my notes and my book and headed up to my room. When I got there, I looked for my watch and wallet and they were not there." "What about your missing room key?" I said. "Uh, yeah, I think I lost my key when I jumped into the pool," he replied. "What type of watch was it, and what did you have in your wallet?" Ron asked. "The watch was a TAG Heuer, and my wallet had a couple of credit cards, my driver's license and about $100 bucks."

The questioning went on for several more minutes. It almost took up our entire lunch hour, when, finally, Ron suggested that we call the police and file a formal report. This would help Paul when it comes to insurance replacement and shows that the hotel is doing its due diligence. Paul didn't want the police involved. He was more interested in making sure that he got some cash and a replacement picture I.D. before the training ended on Friday. Ron told us that he would call the police and if/when they needed a statement, he would contact Paul directly.

We headed to the lunch buffet and picked at the scraps that were left over before having to start the afternoon session. The rest of the day went well. No one paid any attention to the fact that Paul and I had disappeared for a while and came into the lunch area together. It's not uncommon for sales people to call customers and handle issues at the office during breaks. Often it takes up our entire breaks and we end up grabbing something to-go to eat back in the classroom.

At our afternoon break, I called our HR department and explained what happened, seeking guidance on how to acquire a picture ID and a potential cash advance for Paul. There were many details involved with that. HR wanted Paul to file a report with them and I made the arrangements to get him to the right people in HR to handle the rest of the paperwork.

The next day, I checked with Paul to see how things went with HR. He said it was fine, and that they would be able to assist. Great! Chalk up another success story to super-trainer. That is, until Thursday rolled around.

The Thursday morning session is always a tough one. It's super-skill day and everyone really needs to "bring it," including the facilitators. You need to dig deep and pull everything you've got to take the previous three days of learning and parlay it into day four. It really works up the appetite, so when lunch came around I was starving. No sooner had I dismissed the class for the lunch break, when Doug, one of the attendees, approached me quietly.

"Can I speak with you privately?" he said. "Of course, absolutely," I replied with concern. He looked a little stressed, his face tight and strained.

"Someone took my Mont Blanc pen. It's an expensive pen and it was given to me as a gift from my dad after I made the first sale of my professional career."

"Are you sure it was stolen? Is it possible that you misplaced it?" I asked.

"I know that it was taken out of the meeting room. I had left it next to my phone and the note pad where I had written down some information from a voice mail message. I left for the restroom, and when I came back, the pen was gone."

"Was anything else missing?" I asked. "No," he replied.

"Are you sure it isn't anywhere in the room, or maybe the restroom? Is it in the pocket of a jacket, or did it roll off behind the table?"

"I looked everywhere. It's nowhere," he replied.

Feeling the twinge of Déjà vu, I spun 180 degrees on my right foot and headed back to the hotel offices. I'm concerned about this news. I'm wondering if there is a problem with the hotel staff. Is someone stealing the guests' valuables? Has the security office received complaints from other guests? I asked Ron about this and he said that the only two guests who reported missing items were the two from my group. He had heard nothing from anyone else.

I left the security office and headed back to the lunch room and pulled Doug aside. "I will speak with the group after lunch. Perhaps someone accidentally picked up your pen, or maybe they've seen it somewhere. If we get nowhere with the group, we can fill out a security report at the hotel security office. Are you okay with that plan?" I asked.

"I'm good," he said, adding, "Thanks for your help."

When the group reconvened after lunch, I addressed everyone asking if they saw the pen. I asked Doug to describe it to the group and show them where he last thought he had placed it. Crickets. Dead silence, as if everyone was keeping some giant secret. I encouraged a response, and no one had seen it.

I asked everyone nicely if it might be possible that someone picked it up by accident and asked if they wouldn't mind checking their personal belongings to see if it was accidentally misplaced. Should anyone find it, please turn it in, no questions asked.

We continued through the session, ending with the instructions for the large group project the following day. The project is a team sales call where they make their final presentation and try to close the sale. Each team is scored points on various criteria such as selling skills, presentation delivery, product knowledge, etc. It's an intense exercise and the teams generally bond together and become good friends. It was the same situation this time around, especially for those who had "Ms. Yes, Ma'am" on their team.

Ms. Yes, Ma'am was a young 25-year-old from a small rural area in the south. She acquired the nickname, Ms. Yes, Ma'am, because she would always answer any female who would address her with "Yes, Ma'am." It was more deliberate than polite. The first few times it sounded charming, but when you are exposed to it day in and day out it gets old. Eventually, you begin to look past the terms of endearment and focus instead on the essence behind the tongue.

It was obvious early on that Ms. Yes, Ma'am was an inexperienced seller. Throughout the course of the week she would emulate the more skilled sellers by implementing their techniques when it was her turn to demonstrate. She came off as a scrappy newbie with a hefty dose of determination and grit.

Ms. Yes, Ma'am was popular with most of the attendees, especially with Paul and Doug. She treated them like big brothers, always asking if she could get them a coffee, or bring back snacks from the break room for them. She learned much about their needs, personal and positional, which helped her gain their trust. It didn't take long for her to get them to help her, including carrying her gigantic backpack to and from the training facility, buying her cocktails after sessions, and helping her hide her lack of skill during role-play and presentation activities.

She also ingratiated herself to one of the other participants, Maria, a local girl, who lived in the area. Ms. Yes, Ma'am and Maria were both on the same presentation team. Maria was a highly skilled B2B sales professional with an equally high emotional intelligence quotient. Ms. Yes, Ma'am was the opposite, as evidenced by her lack of skill and inability to accept constructive feedback and coaching. Her rate of speech was too fast, giving off the appearance of anxious inexperience. As we closed in on the end of the week, Ms. Yes, Ma'am was panicky about having to spend Friday night in a hotel by the airport alone. She was the only attendee who could not get a flight back home until Saturday because she lived in a rural area that is not frequently serviced by the airlines.

Maria, being the kind-hearted leader that she is, stepped up and asked her if she would feel more comfortable staying at her apartment. She would have to sleep on the sofa, but she wouldn't be alone. Ms. Yes, Ma'am happily agreed, thanking Maria up down and sideways for the balance of the afternoon.

Our week-long session ended around 3:00 p.m. on Friday. We concluded the workshop and sent everyone on their way. The facilitators always stay behind for a post-mortem. The debrief is always lively and helpful because I need to send a feedback report on each participant back to the sales manager and general manager. The reports include an overview of their sales persons' participation, their sales strengths and areas for improvement along with some helpful coaching tips. This post-mortem was very interesting. We talked about the thefts, the characters, and of course Ms. Yes, Ma'am.

She was like nothing we've seen before. She was calculating in her approach, as evidenced with her incessant "Yes, Ma'am" salutations, and the doting on her male counterparts. She had a knack for garnering attention, but once she got it she would reveal a tentative posture. She could not grasp the process of making a sale. Not a good fit at all, in fact, she was more of a misfit than a fit. We gave our odds that she would be terminated for non-performance within three months. Chalk it up to bad hiring practice. We finished our business, cleaned up the meeting room and all went our separate ways.

The next morning, Saturday, I received a phone call from Maria. She was about to drop a thunderous bomb.

I answered, "Hello, this is Kathy."

"Kathy, this is Maria, from this week's sales training."

She sounded fearful, speaking slow and low. "I need to tell you what happened last night." She said, "I brought Kiki (a.k.a. Ms. Yes, Ma'am) to my apartment last night because she was scared to stay by herself at the hotel by the airport. She was drinking vodka that she brought with her, and I don't know where she got it from. We watched some TV and started talking about the sales training. She was pretty buzzed and told me some crazy stories. She was making fun of a lot of the salespeople in the class. She told me that she slept with Paul and how easy it was to take his wallet and watch right out from under his nose. She also showed me Doug's Mont Blanc pen, the same one that you asked us about on Thursday after lunch. She slept with him too, so she said. And, from what I gather, she took the pen the night she slept with him. She was proud of this. She started to scare me with her stories. I didn't want her in my apartment, so I called my sister. When my sister called me back, I told Kiki that I had a family emergency and had to leave."

"So, what did you do with her?" I asked.

"I called her a cab to take her to a hotel by the airport, and then I went to my sister's house for the night," she replied.

"Did she show you the wallet and the watch?" I asked.

"No. I don't know if it's a true story or not, but I felt like I needed to call you and let you know."

I ended the conversation by telling her that she was very kind and generous to help Kiki, and that I was sorry that it had turned out the way it did. I also told her that I would need to report what she told me to HR and that they will investigate, which will most likely require her to make a statement and probably be interviewed.

Ms. Yes, Ma'am was quite the Lucifer Leader. Now that you've had a moment to digest her story, let's talk about what we can learn from it.

First, can you believe it? It sounds crazy, right? How can a company operate with such hiring practices? The job description states the requirement of a college degree; I spoke with the sales manager during the workshop and asked how he found his new hire; he told me that he recruited her from behind a cosmetic counter at the mall. When I asked him why he selected this candidate he told me that talent was limited in his area and he felt that she demonstrated the hutzpah that would serve her well in outside B2B sales. She must have got him hook, line and sinker at "Yes, Sir." I disagree with the reasoning behind his hiring decision, but then again, I've just spent a week with Ms. Yes Ma'am.

Do you have someone like this working in your organization? Someone who was hired because of a gut feeling from the hiring manager? Someone who plays the role of the underdog who over-uses terms of endearment to create an air of sincerity?

> **Do you have someone like this working in your organization? Someone who was hired because of a gut feeling from the hiring manager?**

The nonprofit Fraud Victim Advocacy Group describes how con artists seek out the needy. They hunt until they find someone who has an unfulfilled desire that even they themselves may be unaware of until the carrot is dangled in front of their face. The con artist is masterful at finding their marks. They use some serious skill to earn your confidence to gain access to your trust, your good will, and your compassion to carry out their fraudulent plans. One of their most masterful skills is their ability to "blend in" and become a part of the community. Our little underdog Lucifer was a masterful mocking-bird, quickly learning the language of her peers. Using her power of insight, she keenly developed the personal and positional needs of her colleagues and leveraged those needs to affect her relationships with them. And that was the foundation from which she could open her window of opportunity.

Despite her ability to legitimize her place in "the tribe," there was still something *off* about her. But, being the kind, accepting, compassionate people that we are, we turned a blind eye to the tell-tale signs and walked right in to her master plan.

⫸🔥 LUCIFER LESSON #1 🔥⫷
Follow Established Hiring Practices

If the pre-hire sales assessment returns a score below the cut, don't go to bat for an exception.

If the pre-hire sales assessment returns a score below the cut, don't go to bat for an exception. By the way, did I mention that she didn't have a college degree? A degree was a job requirement! In my role as Director of Sales Training, I was the principal keeper of the data and analysis of our pre-hire assessment. Yes, it was a validated assessment, meaning that our assessment provider carefully collected data on our high performers and the low performers. Then, they created the assessment and the cut score accordingly, and they tested it against actual performance.

If the sales manager wants to hire someone who does not make the cut, they have to get approval from "the higher-ups." This should be a part of the approval process required of the sales manager to submit their rationale for why senior management should waive the requirement. In several cases, the sales managers were granted their requests. I tracked the performance of hires above and below the cut score. Part of my job was to send a monthly report that showed sales productivity against the cut score. Those who were hired below the cut score underperformed in the first three months after hire. More importantly, though, is that the assessment tied questions back to the company's guiding values, which translated to organizational fit in addition to behaviors that rated with high performers.

Therefore, if you scored below the cut, you weren't a good fit with the company culture. So, my recommendation is to use a pre-hire assessment and make sure that it is weighted well for organizational fit and not just rated for sales productivity behaviors. For tips on using pre-hire assessments visit www.luciferleaders.com.

⚞ LUCIFER LESSON #2 ⚟
Own Onboarding

It's important to look under the hood and kick the tires before the test drive.

Ms. Yes, Ma'am was hired into a branch location where there are no sales people; she was the only one. She had no role models. The sales manager was located remotely and provided little supervision and guidance. How was he supposed to know that she was not capable of doing the job without the benefit of observation and just plain old-fashioned sales management? It's important to look under the hood and kick the tires before the test drive. The behaviors that Swindler Lucifer demonstrated in sales training would have been realized a lot earlier if the manager was more present. For tips on long-distance onboarding visit www.luciferleaders.com.

⚞ LUCIFER LESSON #3 ⚟
The Sales Trainer Safety Net

Would the sales manager have been able to make a difference if he was constantly reinforcing the guiding values? No. Would he have been able to make a difference if he was reinforcing the importance of the work to be done? No. But, he would have realized the hiring mistake before spending the money sending her to sales training. This is where the keen eye of the sales trainer can step in as the safety net. The trainers saw the behavior. We knew it wasn't a fit. But, this little Lucifer caught the sales manager's eye. He sensed a certain level of "hutzpah" that he thought would carry through to performance. He's thinking that he did well. Sales Managers have pride in their new hires. After all, they've invested a lot of time in the recruitment process.

The "halo effect" is alive and well in the initial weeks during the honeymoon period. The manager has a certain degree of bias that their selection is a good one. In the case of Swindler Lucifer, it was not. I know one of the best sales trainers in the business and she always says, "How do you tell a sales manager that his baby is ugly?" The answer lies in in the relationship between sales training and sales management. If you are a sales trainer, build relationships with your sales managers. Earn their respect as a trusted advisor, so when the need arises, you can have a frank conversation with the sales manager. He'll know you have his back, and you'll save him a lot of grief in the long run.

> If you are a sales trainer, build relationships with your sales managers. Earn their respect as a trusted advisor, so when the need arises, you can have a frank conversation with the sales manager. He'll know you have his back, and you'll save him a lot of grief in the long run.

⟐ LUCIFER LESSON #4 ⟐
Follow the Lines That Lead to Lucifer

When the sales trainers conducted the facilitator debrief, we all agreed that we observed an individual who was not capable of doing the job, but shrewd enough to use what she observed from others to win her teammates' mindshare and advance her position as an underdog, conning those around her and engaging in her deviant behavior. She secured the appearance of being willing to make the incremental improvements necessary to evolve into a better sales rep. Those actions rallied the others around her to a position of support. Like an Agatha Christie novel, she lured her marks under different pretexts. One by one they become complicit in supporting her deviant behavior.

⟐ LUCIFER LESSON #5 ⟐
Confidence Pro

Sales is a magnet for the confidence pro. They gravitate toward the profession as an easy way to make a buck. The difference between a true sales professional and a confidence pro might be as simple as a walk through the resume. The con does not stick around for long. They move around a lot. They are job hoppers. They play the part for as long as they can before they are found out. They are intense sales people who bully their way into the sale, using high pressure sales tactics.

A quick way to smoke out a con during the interview process is to ask them to tell you about a time when they had difficulty getting to a prospective decision maker. What did they do to get the prospect to take their call? Listen for answers that would indicate that they misled the prospect. Things like, "I left a voice message telling the prospect that I heard something about them from one of their competitors," or (seriously, I've heard this one before), "I pretend that I'm a brother, sister or cousin, with an important message." Yikes!

> **A quick way to smoke out a con during the interview process is to ask them to tell you about a time when they had difficulty getting to a prospective decision maker. What did they do to get the prospect to take their call?**

Hiring managers, think about this: If you have a lot of customer defection from a specific sales person who has a long history of job hopping, take a closer look. You might have a Lucifer Leader on your hands!

HIDDEN COSTS FROM SWINDLER LUCIFER

So, what were the hidden costs with this Lucifer Leader? We already know about the hard costs of the termination associated with salary, benefits, pre-hire and training costs. In this case, Swindler Lucifer's hard costs added up to $23,550. Now, let's add in the soft cost. First, there was the cost of the training facilitator and HR and Accounting to triangulate efforts to secure identification and funds for Paul to carry out the week and get home, $515. Next was the time spent with hotel security for both thefts, $463, which included the salaries for the facilitator, the two trainees, the security director and for the administration of the paperwork. Next was transportation of Ms. Yes, Ma'am from Maria's house to the airport hotel and the cost of the airport hotel and subsequent transportation to the airport, $340.

Throw in the Tag Hauer watch and the Mont Blanc Pen, $2,540. Add the investigation by HR, which included internal legal, outside legal counsel, and time spent by finance, senior sales management and the president of the company, $110,000. Total cost for Swindler Lucifer is $137,408.

CHAPTER FOUR

Criminal Lucifer

There are Lucifer Leaders who are natural born deviants and eventually evolve into full blown criminals in their adult life. If you are reading this, you probably have come across one of these folks in your professional career. In sales, it's the Lucifer who forges signatures on company contracts, gets paid the commission, and flies the coop before anyone notices. It's the Lucifer who sells cocaine out of the company car and in local taverns and sports bars. In some way, shape or form, they use the company as a fine-tuned organized crime syndicate for their secondary enterprise. This Lucifer nearly cost the company its brand, and that my friends, can destroy a company completely. This is the story of Criminal Lucifer.

> **The Criminal Lucifer uses the company as a fine-tuned organized crime syndicate for their secondary enterprise.**

One really must wonder about an adult sales professional who travels for business and arrives at a week-long sales training workshop, half-way across the country, with no credit cards and no cash. Two words: Red Flag.

It was Monday, day-one of sales training. The agenda included a group dinner on the first night as a meet and greet type of event. We invited various directors and executives to the dinner to mingle with the group and make them feel welcomed. But, for this dinner, the directors and executives were all out of town, so we were on our own. As we were getting ready to load the group on the transportation van, one of the attendees named Chris approached me and told me that he needed a favor.

It turns out that Chris allegedly left his cash and credit cards at home on his dresser when he left for the airport on Sunday. He did not realize it until he got to the airport and tried to buy a cup of coffee. Since there wasn't enough time for him to go back home to retrieve it, or enough time for his wife to drive it to the airport, he made arrangements for his wife to overnight a personal check to the corporate office so that he could cash it at a local bank to have ample funds to make it through the week and get him back home.

The "favor" he needed from me was for me to run him over to a bank on the way back to the hotel so that he could cash the check. It didn't seem too much to ask, and it would be a quick stop on the way, so I agreed. To make sure that everyone else was taken care of, I selected Joe, an account manager from the Midwest, to serve as leader and shepherd of the group. I gave him the name of hotel banquet manager and asked him if he would kindly get everyone seated in the hotel restaurant, order some appetizers for the table, and that I would be there shortly with Chris after we get done at the bank.

The van took off, and I drove Chris to the bank around the corner. Everything seemed to be going according to plan until Chris emerged from the bank fifteen minutes later and told me that they would not cash the out-of-state check. He then suggested that we stop at a grocery store because they might be more likely to cash the check. So, I drove Chris to a grocery store. I waited in the car for another 15 minutes. Again, no cash. I suggested that we head to the hotel, because as a guest of the hotel they will cash the personal check. While that made sense to me, Chris suggested that since we are on our way to the hotel if we could make just one more stop, at a check cashing place, he would have one more opportunity to cash the check before he would no longer have the convenience or generosity of my transportation mobility. Ugh, ok. I gave in, found a currency exchange and waited another 15 minutes. He got into my car and told me that they cashed his check, but for a hefty fee, and that he was now a proud "member" of this currency exchange.

By then we were arriving at the hotel more than an hour late. We walked in, and he headed to his room to drop off his back pack while I headed directly to the restaurant. As soon as I got through the front door, Sylvia, the waitress assigned to serve our group, came running toward me in a bit of a panic.

I've known Sylvia for many years, as we have been using this property for a long time. Sylvia is a loyal hotel employee and very customer service oriented. She always has my back. She makes sure that all my guests are happy, and that any visiting dignitaries from the corporate office are attended to promptly, and keeps all my group events humming.

I was perplexed at her state of panic, and as she was hurrying toward me from behind the bar and past the pool table, my mind started racing through a litany of possible situations: Did someone get hurt?

Choke? Did they break something? Start a fight? I probably thought about every scenario inside of the 10 seconds it took her to reach me.

As she approached she whispered, "Miss Kathy, your group has spent $700 already and they haven't even ordered dinner yet!" She continued, "The big man, Joe, told me that you gave him permission to order while they wait for you to come back from the bank. I am so sorry, I should have waited for you."

Sylvia showed me the tab. Low and behold, they have been ordering top shelf booze, by the bucket, for the last hour. When I say top shelf, I'm talking very expensive single malt scotch and liqueurs, stuff that goes for $25 a glass. They also ordered enough appetizers to feed a small army. The actual ticker tape was almost 24 inches long. I told Sylvia to cut them off, serve no more drinks or food, and that I will close out the tab and send everyone to their rooms. Good grief, like children.

Just as I began to digest this, I saw one of the attendees, Toni, walking toward me like a zombie. She was carrying a tall beer glass that was filled to the very top with Chartreuse. If you aren't familiar, Chartreuse is a French liqueur that casts a yellow-green color that looks a lot like anti-freeze. It has a very strong taste, both spicy and pungent. It clocks in at 110-proof.

Toni was wobbling on her too-high heels and the Chartreuse was sloshing around, spilling over the edges of the glass on to her hand and wrist and just about everywhere else. Although Toni appeared to be walking toward me, and looking right at me, she was oblivious that I was there at all. As I passed her, I told her that the dinner is over and to go to her room. I doubted that she noticed.

I headed toward the space where the private dinners are held and turned the corner to walk down another aisle of the restaurant when I saw Joe. He was all happy coming toward me, welcoming me to the dinner like a happy puppy on the return of the master. Suddenly, I realized that his crotch was flashing bright, electrified primary colors from inside his pants. As it turned out, the marketing department gave all the attendees rubber super balls, that when bounced, flash bright lights that look like a colorful lightning storm. My selected leader, the appointed shepherd, got buzzed, fueled the demise of the team, and then as a joke bounced the super ball to electrification and stuck it in his pants! The lights were so bright that they flashed like a cosmic shit storm of disco balls right through the zipper on his fly. A crotch full of red, blue and green lightning bugs! Lovely.

I caught the eye of the bartender, Julio, who's worked at the hotel for years. He's a handsome Mexican-American man who is always wearing top-of-the-line western-wear. His salt and pepper goatee and mustache were perfectly trimmed and played nicely against his full head of silver hair, perfectly coifed for a gentleman of his age. Julio has been a bartender for his entire career, and loves it. He was probably in his mid-sixties or so. His western shirt was custom-made and perfectly starched and pressed. What most patrons don't realize is that he was wearing a very expensive pair of ostrich cowboy boots behind the bar, one of many from his collection. He must be a great bartender to risk wearing such expensive boots in a job where there is a lot of spillage. One thing is for sure, you can tell by his demeanor that he had seen and heard his share of stories in his lifetime. He looked at me with that look, the Cheshire cat look, while he polished stemware. I couldn't wait to get a chance to talk to him, because I was sure he had some nice juicy details about what went down while I was away.

It was the first night, and we had four more to go. From the looks of these people, tomorrow is going to be a long and unproductive day. I paid the tab and headed over to the bar to have a sit-down with Julio. There's nothing like a good bartender to dish the night away. Sure enough, he was just as I left him, polishing stemware. Julio and I go way back; he's served many of the groups that I have brought to the restaurant. I took a seat close to where the wait staff drop off and pick up orders. Julio began the conversation.

"That is some group you're managing this week. You've got your hands full."

"So, what can you tell me about what went down while I was away?" I said.

"The big guy directed everyone to their seats and led the decision-making around the appetizers." Julio continued, "But then one of the gals spoke up and corralled the group into a game of beer pong using some sort of superball that flashed lights when it hit the table."

"Those balls are heavy; they aren't like ping-pong balls, they could cause damage if they hit the side of a glass," I said.

"And that it did," Julio responded. "The shots they ordered were served in short rocks glasses, and they knocked over a few."

"Did any of them break?" I asked. "No, but they knocked a few over and spilled some pricy booze that I did not replace for free." He continued, "I told them no ball playing in the house."

As I filed the facts Julio provided, I thanked him for his intel and headed home to put together my "dress 'em down" speech. Not a good way to start off the week.

The next morning was not pretty. Ms. Chartreuse looked as green as her cocktail from the night before. She moved the small trash can next to her seat. Mr. Flashpants apologized up and down and attempted to return his superball to me; I did not want to touch it. The condition of the others varied depending on the amount of their participation the night before. There were lots of Cokes, Sprites, Dr. Peppers and Mt. Dew cans on the tables ... shocking. As I scanned the room, I noticed someone was missing. Where's Mr. Check Cash? He's late. I asked the group if anyone has seen Chris. No one. The last time I saw him was when he headed straight to his room to drop off his back pack. Come to think of it, I never saw him come back to the restaurant, and I was there for about 45 minutes. I'll deal with that later. For now, it's time to get down to business.

I began with a serious tone:

As sales professionals representing our company, you are expected to observe the highest standards of ethical behavior and conduct yourself with the utmost integrity throughout your attendance at this training function.

You will treat your colleagues and your trainers with courtesy and respect. You are expected to act with tolerance, sensitivity, respect, and impartiality toward other persons' cultures and backgrounds. You are expected to follow classroom rules and directions, be prepared for class, be attentive, do your best work, respect other learners, and be on time. You are accountable for completing tasks that are assigned in the classroom, and you are expected to exercise adequate control over matters for which you are responsible. You will refrain from participating in any activity that might interfere with your ability to complete your training. You will strive to take reasonable care to ensure your own health and safety and avoid any behaviors that would adversely

*affect the safety of others. Any deviation from this standard will result
in immediate termination and possible legal action.*

And, I can probably tack on the following for use at every session:
Thou shall not get drunk every night. Thou shall not attend the
session with a hangover. Thou shall not whine. Thou shall not ask
the trainer for a ride to the liquor store. Thou shall not ask for special
seating. Thou shall not ask permission to leave early. Thou shall
not return the clothes that you specifically purchased to wear to the
training event. Thou shall not text message your boyfriend during
class. Thou shall not wear a thong as an undergarment. Thou shall
not show one's belly button. Thou shall not "do" every gal in the
training class. Thou shall not argue with the trainer. Thou shall not
"stir the pot" with other participants. Thou shall not pick-up strangers
in the bar and proudly announce the company you work for. Thou
shall not make fun of other attendees. Thou shall not constantly
complain about jet lag, etc., etc., etc.

I scared the bejesus out of them, at least for the time being. They were
all sitting up straight, as best they could and we began the day. Guess
who walked in the door? Yes, Mr. Check Cash.

"You're late," I said as he took his seat.

"Yes, sorry," he replied.

"Why are you late?" I asked in front of the entire room.

"I had to wire some of the money back into my checking account
at home. Turns out that my wife miscalculated how much we
had in the bank when she overnighted the check. I had to cover
the overdraft."

He's not hung over and he responded effortlessly. But, that sure sounded like a bunch of BS to me. I'm going to keep my eyes on this guy.

The week progressed without much drama. Extra-curricular socializing was off limits since the fiasco on Monday, so productivity had increased overall. The only suspect behavior was around Chris. I learned that he disappeared for most of the group homework assignment on Thursday night. He gave the team some cockamamie story about getting lost downtown after meeting up with an old friend. Not fair to the team and they rewarded him for it handsomely by assigning him the toughest part of the project prep and delivery. It hurt the team in the end. Chris delivered less than stellar performance for the team and cost them a win. But, it was a team building experience for those who worked together in the absence of their lame team member.

I was glad when the session was over and everyone left. It was a tough week. I began the process of writing out the feedback and coaching letters for the sales managers. I cleaned up the meeting room and spent some time reflecting.

The weeks and months moved on, and we continued with the workshops. About three months after "Flashpants," I learned that our office where Mr. Check Cash worked was raided by the FBI. It turned out that Chris was involved in an organized check cashing ring. The overnight envelope that his wife sent to him did not have "*a* check" in it. As a matter of fact, it had *several* checks in it: one for each stop we made on our way to the hotel, and then some. They walked him out of the office in handcuffs.

This Lucifer cost the company a bundle to the tune of $563,877 in hiring and recruiting costs, training cost, lost productivity and legal fees associated with the investigation to clear the company of any wrong-doing.

So, what did we learn from this? Well, first, this hire scored very high on the pre-hire assessment. In so doing, he appeared to be a shooting star. The manager rushed him through the hiring process and neglected to complete the background check. He passed the drug test, but the background check was delayed and then never happened. Had that one component of our hiring process followed through, we may have been able to save face and human capital investment as this was not this guy's first rodeo. It happens all the time: parts of the workflow get skipped, rushed, omitted, neglected, glossed over. All in the name of a good gut feeling.

When you stop and think about it, a criminal on your team isn't that hard to miss. Why? Because they are pre-occupied. They have a side-gig that is way more important than work and cannot be interrupted by the mundane activities of a sales professional. In an article featured in *Forbes,* "More than 75% of frauds occur in six departments: accounting, operations, sales, executive upper management, customer service and purchasing."[1] So, if you have someone on your team who disappears from time to time, is always making excuses for their lack of performance, and don't seem to contribute much to the overall productivity of the team, you might have a Criminal Lucifer on your hands.

---

1   "How Do You Spot the Thief Inside Your Company" by Marc Webber Tobias, Contributing Writer, *Forbes*, December 21, 2012.

When you stop and think about it, a criminal on your team isn't that hard to miss. Why? Because they are pre-occupied. They have a side-gig that is way more important than work and cannot be interrupted by the mundane activities of a sales professional.

➤ LUCIFER LESSON #1 ≈
The Hiring Process

Follow the hiring process. Don't skip mundane,
but extremely important steps.

Follow the hiring process. Don't skip mundane, but extremely important steps. How many times have you hired someone *before* completing the background and drug checks? How many of those checks slipped through the cracks because you got too busy to follow-up and get it done? Besides, the new hire seems okay, right? The steps in the hiring process are there for a reason and in this case, a half-million dollars-worth of reasons.

➤ LUCIFER LESSON #2 ≈
Enforce Consequences

Don't put up with poor behavior that does not meet the standards
and expectations established for the group.

Don't put up with poor behavior that does not meet the standards and expectations established for the group. If someone is late, enact discipline immediately. Don't let it slide. Enforce the consequences. If you are a trainer, make sure that the expectations are established before the attendees arrive at the training session. I am a huge proponent and card-carrying member of *The Six Disciplines of Breakthrough Learning*.[2] I require specific pre-work for each workshop that I facilitate. Part of the pre-work requires the manager to sit down and discuss the objectives of the workshop with the attendee and draw a clear line of sight to the outcomes of the training. I want to make sure that the attendee knows exactly why they are attending the training and what their specific focus should include when they are in the classroom. Before I got my "6D" religion, standard operating procedure was to ask attendees to state their objective during the workshop opening. Invariably, we would hear, "because my boss told me that I had to attend." Or, "I won't get my sign bonus until I complete the training." That's a clear sign of zero engagement.

If you are the trainer, make sure that you are in alignment with HR and field sales management on the behavioral expectations of the attendees. As a training facilitator, you need the latitude to enact discipline in your classroom. At the very least, have a procedure for escalating discipline for behavior that does not meet expectations. To learn more about how I use The Six Disciplines of Breakthrough Learning in my practice, visit www.kknowhow.com.

---

2   Roy V.H. Pollock, Andy Jefferson, Calhoun W. Wick, *The Six Disciplines of Breakthrough Learning: How to Turn Training and Development into Business Results*, (Hoboken, NJ: John Wiley & Sons, 2015). *[Please confirm that this is correct, because the 6D's appear to predate the book and there is a 6D's Company.]*

⚡ LUCIFER LESSON #3 ⚡
See Something/Say Something

If it looks peculiar, acts peculiar and smells peculiar, it's probably peculiar. Ask questions and seek to understand. Establish a "see something, say something" protocol at work. According to the Association of Certified Fraud Examiners' 2014 report, 40% of occupational fraud was detected because of a tip.[3] So, create a policy and make sure everyone is aware of it. Open a tip-line to help you identify potential problems.

HIDDEN COSTS FROM CRIMINAL LUCIFER

Criminal Lucifers can cost your company a bundle. It probably won't come as a surprise where the hidden costs can be found in this case: legal fees and investigative procedure costs. When an employee gets arrested for a check-cashing scheme on your premises, you are responsible for defending yourself, your company and your other employees. That requires an investigation and the employment of legal counsel to make sure that all the bases are covered. In some cases, your company can be responsible for the bad behavior of an employee. Background checks are imperative to keep you out of hot water, and even then, you still must spend a small fortune to defend yourself.

---

3   Association of Certified Fraud Examiners "Report to The Nations on Occupational Fraud and Abuse 2014 Global Fraud Study."

CHAPTER FIVE

Libertine Lucifer

While it is not uncommon for a Lucifer to come across as an odd duck, when it comes to histrionic personality disorder, it transforms the odd duck into an extrovert who is completely taken by their self-perceived magnetic personality. The irony is that while they see themselves as charismatic and captivating, everyone else views them as attention-seeking, low self-esteem individuals who don't really belong. They are merely tolerated by virtue of being part of the group. Their disorder comes with a cost, and in this case, $118,000. This is the story of Libertine Lucifer.

> The irony is that while a Libertine Lucifer sees themselves as charismatic and captivating, everyone else views them as attention-seeking, low self-esteem individuals who don't really belong.

This training session was going to be special because there would be three business leaders from another continent attending as our guests. I had been working with and corresponding with the team over the past year, assisting them with talent development questions. But this would be my first professional exposure to a truly global experience in the classroom. I made sure that I did my homework; I researched the cultural aspects of face-to-face relationship building and the selling/negotiating approach in their culture. I felt prepared with my new found understanding of our cultural differences, and I modified the training materials and activities to meet the needs of this culturally diverse classroom. In addition to my own preparation, I wanted to prepare the domestic attendees' cultural awareness so that they could adapt their behavior to embrace the differences of our cross-cultural friends.

The session kicked off with a buzz in the air. The domestic attendees were excited to meet the members from far away and vice versa. We began, as we usually do, with an ice-breaker. This was my opportunity to prepare the American sales reps for cultural awareness, and at the same time make our visitors feel welcome and find some common ground. As the icebreaker proceeded, we learned that one of the foreign attendees spoke no English, one could understand and speak a little English, and one was very fluent in English and acted as translator. This would prove to be no problem for the week's activities. I kept the three in their own triad for the week so that they could work on their skills and on the simulations within the context of their sales and negotiation culture.

During the icebreaker, one of the foreign attendees made a joke about his objective for the workshop, which was translated by the English-fluent attending member: "He said that he wouldn't mind finding an American wife." It was said with humble respect and delivered with perfect punch. It came across as cute, and the class got a good chuckle out of it. One attendee in particular sat up and took notice of the comment. She was a local from an office close to the facility where we were holding the workshop. As such, she drove to the facility, but stayed at the hotel like the others. Having a car on the property gave her a freedom that the others did not have, and a power that others wanted. This fed her attention-seeking personality.

It didn't take long for Ms. Libertine's disorder to kick into high gear. No sooner did our foreign attendee make his proclamation did Libertine Lucifer begin sending flirtatious glances his way. She went full-on with her attention to our special guest regardless of the language barrier. She was a bit older than the other attendees, neither attractive or unattractive, but definitely "rough around the edges"; her actions were noticeable due to her lack of decorum.

The first day went off without a hitch. The group was on their own for dinner. I overheard Libertine Lucifer coordinating her minions to go out to dinner. I didn't pay too much attention but managed to get in a comment about being able to walk to a number of excellent dining options across the street to keep the group close by. My experience was that group outings that stray too far from the hotel never end on a high note.

I packed up my briefcase and got ready to head home for the evening. I stopped by the front desk to request additional water for the next day. Surprise, surprise: The front desk had a message for me to contact the event manager when convenient. Sometimes I wonder if I can ever get through one of these sessions without any issues.

I walked back to the management section and peeked my head inside the event manager's office. I love this event manager. She is a pistol; very outgoing, jovial, and highly customer oriented.

"Hey, Shondra," I said as I interrupted her concentration on whatever she was working on.

"Hey KK, how did your session go today?" she asked.

"Pretty good, considering that 20% of the class does not speak any English. The front desk gave me a message that you wanted to talk to me about something."

"Yup," she said. "I wanted to give you a head's-up that one of your attendees used valet parking upon check-in. When we tried to collect the $25, she told us that she was told that all parking was included in the contract. So, we gently told her that it was not included in the contract, and that we would bring it to your attention so that you could adjust your communication properly."

"Well, isn't that special," I said with a sarcastic Dana Carvey Church Lady accent. "Just an FYI, I specifically communicated that all incidentals are covered by the individual. Why would she use valet service when your garage is 20 feet away and free for the guests?" I continued with a brief commentary on the insolence of some people, when Shondra gently interrupted.

"Wait, there's more," she said. "She ordered two bottles of Dom Perignon from room service."

"Well, did you charge her personal credit card?" I asked.

"When your gal checked in, she did not leave a credit card with the front desk. She told us that she accidentally left it at home and she asked her brother to drive it up. Apparently, she lives a couple of hours south of here." Shondra added, "Since we knew she would be here all week, we said we would wait for her credit card."

I said to Shondra, "So, you are expecting to get a card from her tonight, right?"

"Correct," she replied. "I'll let you know what happens." I then headed home to grab a bite, finish checking my emails, and get ready for the next day.

The next day was to begin with the regional vice president kicking off the session. I got there extra early to make sure that everything was buttoned up. The attendees were filtering in from breakfast with their coffees and leftovers. I caught a glimpse of Libertine Lucifer out of the corner of my eye and made a mental note to check in with Shondra and re-affirm our incidental expense policy with the offender. She was telling quite a story as several attendees were circled around her listening to the details of whatever it was she was explaining. If I wasn't so busy coaching the RVP, I would have loved to eavesdrop on her conversation. I just cannot imagine what she could possibly drone on about that could be so interesting to people that are still somewhat strangers.

I got everyone settled in, got the RVP staged to my left and kicked off the session. I introduced the RVP, talked him up big about his commitment to sales training and the respect he has for professional sales people. He was a nice man, a former ranking officer in the military. He was fair and approachable, and always seemed to return good bottom-line results.

It's always a double-edged sword when the visiting dignitaries come by to talk to the group. They ask for thirty minutes and take ninety. The first thirty minutes is used up by asking each person in the room to introduce themselves, where they are from, their sales experience, what drew them to the company, etc. This round had the added complication of the foreign contingent. We are always pressed for time, so these things can really throw me off for the balance of the day. The other edge of the sword is that I get to sit for the duration, a nice long break to kick-start the day.

Most of the time I'm seated in the back of the room, but on this occasion I was seated to the right side of the room with full view of the audience. I like this angle because I can read the expressions on the attendees' faces. You can gather a lot of intel on people from their posture and their reactions. I scanned the room and saw variations of ass-kissing interest, compelling note taking, nodding heads, doodlers, and of course a distractor, Libertine Lucifer. She was seated directly across from the RVP. She was seated with her right leg bent under her left leg. She had her shoes off and was diligently picking at the callouses on the heel of her right foot; engrossed and staring blankly at the RVP. I could see the chunks of dead skin dropping to the mosaic carpet. I think I even heard them hit the floor. I'm not sure that anyone else noticed, but I think the RVP did. I caught him looking at her a couple of times. Yup, I was thinking, another fine hiring decision! I wondered what she does in front of the customer?

Finally, the fireside chat was over, and he opened it up for questions. Some of the folks had questions. Some had pretty good questions. Others stayed silent. Libertine Lucifer just stared blankly. It was a little over an hour total. The RVP said his goodbyes, and the suck-ups raced to shake his hand on his way out. We took a break.

During the break I meandered over to the management office and poked my head past Shondra's door.

"Well?" I said. "Any progress on the credit card?"

Shondra replied, "Nope. She said that for sure it was coming tonight. In the meantime, she added another valet service to her tab and two more bottles of Dom Perignon and a chocolate covered strawberry platter."

"That sounds extravagant, and expensive," I said. "Why did you guys let her charge that?"

"My night shift did not know the situation, and when they noticed that there was no card on file, they did deny the service, but she's a pretty good schmoozer. She told them the whole story about the brother and must have been pretty convincing because my night manager approved it." Shondra added, "The incidentals tab for her is up to $635."

"I haven't had a chance to talk to her yet because we had an RVP come in this morning. I will talk to her at the next break," I said, and then I left and returned to the general session room. We got in what we could do with the time we had left before the lunch break. Throughout the rest of the morning, Libertine Lucifer was all over her foreign friend. She invaded his space whenever she got the chance. She interrupted often with grand gestures, vying to be the center of attention.

When we broke for lunch, I cornered Libertine Lucifer and told her that valet parking and other incidentals are not covered in the contract, and that she needs to pay for what she ordered. She gave me the same song and dance that she regurgitated to the hotel for the past two nights. I urged her to take care of the situation immediately. She promised that the brother was on his way, and we left for lunch.

The remainder of the session continued throughout the week. By the time Friday came around, Libertine Lucifer had not yet submitted her credit card to the hotel. When the session concluded, she promptly left the hotel and stuck me with the $635 bill. It will be charged back to her office, which won't make the GM very happy, but the GM knows the rules.

As soon as I cleaned up the meeting room and finished the feedback to the sales managers, I called Libertine Lucifer's manager and explained what had happened. He was pissed, to say the least. He revealed that the company gave her a week to get it paid. She was fired on the following Friday.

So, what did we learn from Libertine Lucifer? Let's break it down:

～🔥 LUCIFER LESSON #1 🔥～
Behavior-Based Interviewing

If it walks like an odd duck, and quacks like an odd duck, chances are, it's an odd duck. There isn't a pre-hire assessment in the world that can take the place of an experienced manager executing a good behavioral-based interview. Sure, the assessment can predict a specific outcome, but they are best used in conjunction with an experienced team of interviewers who can tease out the scope of the individual's performance regarding culture and the all-around "wholeness" of the candidate.

> **When a pre-hire assessment comes back positive, and yet the presentation doesn't match the pre-conceived notion of what presents itself as normal," that's a disconnect: A Red Flag!**

When a pre-hire assessment comes back positive, and yet the presentation doesn't match the pre-conceived notion of what presents itself as normal," that's a disconnect: A Red Flag! When that happens, you need to dig. But, if you're in a hurry to hire, and the assessment returns a positive score, it's easy to dummy-down on the face-to-face interview.

Interviewing is hard. You need to completely understand your objectives for the interview both inside and outside the context of the assessment. You need to be prepared for things you spot during the face-to-face, and to be ready to ask questions that might not be in your prepared interview plan: questions that can address something that you see, sense or feel. With Libertine Lucifer, the sales manager observed flirtatious behavior during the interview.

What might he be able to ask to understand the behavior he is observing, without getting him in legal hot water? Ask the person to describe a time when their work was criticized or disapproved of? Listen keenly and press for the specific situation or task that was criticized, the action the applicant took, and the result.

Know that a Libertine Lucifer is uber-sensitive to criticism. Ask them to describe a time when they worked on a team where credit was given to a team member who wasn't deserving. The Libertine Lucifer will display exaggerated emotions and a hefty dose of drama in their response. Because they need to be the center of attention, they tend to believe that relationships are more than they really are, they have low emotional intelligence, and they come across as overtly suggestive.

Another question to help identify a Libertine Lucifer is this: "Tell me about a time when you had to adjust to a colleague's working style to complete a project or achieve your objectives." That will raise the hackles on the back of the neck of the Libertine Lucifer. They *can't* adjust. They *don't* adjust.

∼≥ LUCIFER LESSON #2 ≤∼
Nip It in the Bud

Nip it in the bud early on. I learned about the missing credit card on Day One, but I did not confront Libertine until Day Three. In hindsight, I should have confronted her immediately and informed her that I would be notifying her sales manager. Would it have stopped the behavior? Maybe. Maybe not. Would it have offended the new hire and potentially risked a voluntary termination? Maybe. For the Libertine Lucifer, yes, it would be highly offensive, but at the same time, she would be the center of attention, and exiting the organization would not serve her personality disorder. One would think that if it was truly an oversight, leaving the credit card at home, the new hire would be apologizing up and down, and would get it corrected immediately, taking ownership of the problem. If, on the other hand, the deed was nefarious, then by nipping it in the bud we would realize soon enough the nature of the individual at hand.

Additionally, the sales manager gave Libertine Lucifer a week to pay the outstanding bill. Not a good move. The extra week provided plenty of time for more damage. Who knows what she could have run off with, let alone the extra week of salary that we had to pay to her. The manager should have demanded the payment immediately.

This is not a great way to start your career with a company, but if your intentions are to take advantage, to steal or to cheat, it won't matter who gets tough with you. It doesn't faze the likes of a Libertine Lucifer.

HIDDEN COSTS FROM LIBERTINE LUCIFER

So, where are the hidden costs? On the surface, it looks like we lost out on all the hard costs associated with pre-hire, which includes the costs to recruit, administer the pre-hire assessment, background check and drug test, $2,875, BAM! Add to that hiring, training, salary and benefits, lost to this Lucifer $19,330, double-BAM! Tack on the superficial costs associated with the room service, champagne and valet parking; we're up to $22,840. But, where are the hidden costs? If you guessed lost opportunity costs, you're right! She sold nothing in the remaining week on the job, which translates into $1,800 of revenue multiplied by the remaining weeks in the year comes out to a loss of $77,500. If you guessed the cost of the sales manager having to deal with the situation and taking his time away from revenue-generating activities, you're right, to the tune of $2,300, not to mention the additional cost to fill the vacancy , OOPS, there goes another $7,500 (if we're lucky)! And, what about the little detail called unemployment insurance? She was fired. She will apply for unemployment. The company will likely contest it and the burden of proof is on the employer, which requires the involvement of the company employment attorney, filling out the forms, the back and forth of a contested case, BAM, add another $4,260. If you guessed the cost of the trainer and the hotel personnel chasing down the details, you're right, $3,600 for a grand total of $118,000!! And, don't forget the cost of the reputation of the sales office, what will that end up costing? Will the staff survive or thrive from the defection of this Lucifer Leader? Let's ponder that for a moment ... her behavior in the classroom was histrionic. She was exhausting in her pursuit for attention. She was not capable of receiving criticism and demonstrated a low Emotional Intelligence quotient. Getting rid of this Lucifer was a healthy move for the entire organization. If you answered that the rest of the team will not only will survive, but thrive, you are right once again!

CHAPTER SIX

Monte Cristo Lucifer

So goes the Lucifer who is the consummate entertainer, the savior-faire, debonair, who has power by virtue of the size of his wallet. People flock around him when money is no object; he alone can afford to seek out the finer things in life and can pay for it. In this case, it seems odd that an individual in this type of sales position would need this type of job if he can freely drop serious coin on high-end food and booze. Is he an eccentric? Maybe he doesn't need the money? Maybe the job is a hobby? A diversion? Nope. It is yet another rendition of a cost of sales to the tune of $370,850. This is the story of Monte Cristo Lucifer.

> **The Monte Cristo Lucifer is the consummate entertainer, the savior-faire, debonair, who has power by virtue of the size of his wallet.**

It was a beautiful spring week. When the weather is splendid, everyone seems to be in a good mood. It's easier to wake up in the morning, you feel more refreshed, and it puts a pep in your step.

This training session was a full class, with sixteen sales reps. We were at a beautiful facility that is walking distance to a paseo lined with boutiques and cafes. The facility itself has rose gardens, an outdoor patio at the pool with a giant fireplace, and a quality restaurant and bar featuring top shelf edibles, liquors and accoutrements. I can tell by the chit chat of the attendees entering the meeting room on day one that they were impressed with the property. For some, a very nice facility shows that the company cares for them and that it's important that they are comfortable. Many attendees are appreciative of the accommodations. Some who come from modest communities around the country are awestruck by the perceived luxury. And of course, there are others who look at the experience as an opportunity.

We began the session, as we do each time, with introductions. The introductions always include a brief background on the individual's experience, and what their objective is for coming to the class. First up is Tamara, a spunky girl who weighs no more than 95 pounds soaking wet. She is very happy to be with the company and to attend the sales training. Her previous experience was selling soap to laundromats. Her objective is to learn as much as she could to bring profitability to the branch and money in her pocket. Next up is Jodi, a poised and stern-mannered rep from a competitor. Her objective is to learn the "new company" way of going to market. Next up is Jason. He has an air of confidence about him. He seems a bit indifferent, yet strident. It is as if he has something to prove, but then again, not. Next is Alison, a mild-mannered girl in her late 20's. She came to the company from the sales department of a national car rental chain. Very polite. Her objective is to learn how to take care of the customer and ensure that she is saying the right thing. The next three, Jimmy, Jeff, and Matt, the "three amigos" as I would later dub them, seemed to know one another even though they came from different parts of the country. My guess was that they met on Sunday during check-in, found common ground, hung out and got to know one another. Jimmy was the alpha-male, easily leading Jeff and Matt. He was the funny guy. Well-dressed, confident and outgoing. He looked athletic. And, he was a suck-up, big time. After gushing about how impressed he was with the degree of experience that the facilitators bring to the classroom, he stated his workshop objective: to be the number one sales person in his office after applying the "top-dog secrets" that we were about to impart to him. Jeff and Matt basically repeated Jimmy's objective as if they had already been programmed to obey. We completed the introductions around the U-shaped table and got down to business.

It will be interesting to see how many hires from this cohort will stick. For whatever reason, this group of salespeople is fixated on product dumping with no palpable selling skills. They are coming from different parts of the country, all with different sales managers. How is it that they are so much alike? Is there a new set of criteria for hiring sales reps that I don't know about? *It's gonna be a long week*, I thought.

We slogged our way through day one and day two. Day three was about to commence when Alison approached me and my co-facilitator in a state of panic. "Oh My God," she said. "Someone charged more than $400 to my room last night." She continued, "They must have gotten my room number, and look, they even forged my signature!"

Great. This is going to be interesting. Is it an inside job or an outside job? Is it someone from inside our cohort, or was it a stranger who took advantage of an opportunity?

Alison stuck out her hand, and in it was a copy of the receipt from the hotel bar with her room number and a forged signature. I looked at the sign-in sheet from day-one to see if I could ascertain if anyone from our group was the culprit. The signature on the receipt did not match that of Alison's. I looked through the list of names and could not for certain match the handwriting from one of the attendees to the signature on the receipt. I'm going to have to take this to hotel management and get some more information.

During the morning break, I asked my co-facilitator if she thought that Alison might be trying to divert a bona-fide charge that she actually made. She thought that Alison was telling the truth. I agreed. I've seen a lot of characters over the years, and I am pretty good at knowing when someone is conning me. Alison just didn't fit the charge. We've dealt with her for two full days already. She is earnest, wanting to do the right thing, and wanting to please. She's a team player, an eager participant and is authentic with her reactions. I won't rule it out entirely, but I can't see Alison as the "perp" on this one.

I took the receipt from Alison with the intention of gathering more facts about the charges from the hotel. I looked over the receipt; pretty standard, top shelf scotch, three steak dinners and six Monte Christos. Odd. What's up with the sandwiches? I mean, I get the scotch and steak, they go together, but what are the sandwiches for? Did several people at this table have Monte Christo sandwiches while the others ate steak? Were the sandwiches for take-out? Things that make you go *Hmmmm* ... I shook my head, placed the receipt in my hotel folder and continued with the session.

During lunch, I headed to the accounting offices at the hotel. I asked the hotel comptroller to help me piece together the facts. It turns out that the bar bill was signed and processed around 12:45 a.m. The receipt originated at the patio bar by the fireplace. All the food and beverages were consumed on the patio.

The patio is very nice. It is adjacent to the outdoor pool, which by the way, is an Olympic-style pool, pristinely clean, and situated against a backdrop of palm trees. There is a huge stone fireplace at the foot of the pool adjacent to the hotel restaurant/bar. There are wrought-iron tables with matching chairs situated on the patio. Hotel patrons frequent the patio for breakfast, lunch and dinner, and occasionally just hang out. It is very inviting, and in fact, I have stopped by a table and sat down many times to jot down a note, collect my thoughts, or just to take a break.

The comptroller told me that the restaurant manager can identify the server and at which table the transaction took place. And, we can interview the server and bartender on duty to collect additional intel. She told me that it wasn't uncommon for signatures to be forged, but generally it usually ends up that it's someone within the group, playing a prank. She doesn't recall any unrelated guest or individual outside of the property being involved in these types of schemes, especially lately.

As it turns out, the perpetrator(s) originated at one of the casual tables off to the side of the fireplace, the one with sofa-style seating and a large round wrought-iron table that sits low like a coffee table rather than a dining table. Unfortunately, the server who waited on the table won't be returning to the restaurant as that was her last shift of her employment. I was assured that the other servers who were around that night who might be helpful in piecing the facts together.

With the help of hotel security and the banquet and sales manager, we approached the bartender who was on duty when the forgery took place. The bar was busy that night, and he barely got a chance to take a break; when he did, it was for "biological reasons" only and immediately returned to the bar. He did not recall seeing any of the individuals at the table where the forgery occurred, but he did recall the orders that were placed and eventually delivered to that table. There was nothing out of the ordinary as he saw it, just another group of businessmen consuming the typical expense report items: scotch, steak and Monte Christos.

What seemed odd to me is that they forged a female name and signature, so surely there must have been a woman with them. Could the server be so preoccupied or apathetic to not notice that a table full of guys signed their bill with the name and room number of a woman, and then turned it in without a second look? The bill was pretty straight-forward; scotch, steak and Monte Christos. There were no dinner salads or wine, or other items that a female would stereotypically order at a dinner. Maybe she had a Monte Christo? But, why so many? There were six on the bill. Why would you eat a steak *and* a Monte Christo? It's not the healthiest food on a menu. It's high in fat, calories and salt. The typical Monte Christo recipe is made of bread, mayo, mustard, ham, turkey and Swiss cheese, and then dipped in a mixture of egg and milk and fried in a pan of grease. I asked if the Monte Christos were ordered "to go." The bartender said that he didn't know if they consumed them on site or took them back to their rooms, or back to wherever they came from.

We didn't get very far with the restaurant staff. It was hard to believe that they did not take more care in verifying a bar tab that exceeded several hundred dollars. It wasn't until later in the day, when I was having a casual conversation with one of trainees, that I learned that the Three Amigos, along with several others, spent a good portion of the previous evening at the patio bar. Normally, I would address the entire group during the workshop and ask if anyone had any infor-mation. But, in this particular case, it was obvious that there was a forgery and possible collusion, so I was certain that I wouldn't get any answers from a group interrogation. Time to reach out to Human Resources.

At the afternoon break, I made a phone call to the HR department, explaining the situation and asking for direction. I spoke with one of our regional HR managers, who is a really good generalist. She always has the right stuff. She told me to run an investigation, make it formal and meet with everyone individually. She told me that it would be best if I can get the hotel to give me a suite where I can run the investigation. Then, she gave me a list of questions to ask each person. The questions were designed to give the impression that I knew more than meets the eye when it came to the facts.

I got the hotel to give me a suite, set up with a table and two chairs set underneath an overhead pendant lamp. Totally Dragnet! Once I secured the interrogation room, I returned to the general session and finished out the day.

The next morning, I collaborated with my co-facilitator and asked her to take the helm of the ship while I completed the investigations. She agreed. As soon as the session was ready to begin, I let the group know that I would be meeting with each person individually. The room where they were to report was suite number 224. I read off a list of names and times, and then proceeded to post the schedule on the wall next to the door that leads from our general session room to the hotel. You can imagine the inquisitive look on their faces. I was sure that they suspected what the conversation would be about, as it had been 24 hours since Alison brought the situation to my attention. She probably told everyone about it by then. A few people asked what they needed to bring with them and what the meeting was about. I told them to bring themselves, and that the one-on-one wouldn't last more than 10 minutes. I had 16 people to interview, and they all had to get done before lunch.

First up was Tamara. I asked her to please follow me up to room 224. As we walk, she asks if this has anything to do with the charges on Alison's room account. Ha! I figured it got around. I responded with, "Yes, it is. This is a serious situation, and I am following company protocol to start the investigative process."

"I didn't have anything to do with it, I swear," she responded. "I just need to ask you a few questions in order to gather the facts," I replied. We continued to walk down the hallway to the elevator and made our way to the appointed suite.

I offered no water, snacks or note paper. I sat Tamera down and began my line of questioning: "Where were you on Tuesday night? Where did you have dinner? Who did you have dinner with? What did you have for dinner? Did you stop by the patio bar? What time? Who did you see from our class? Where were they sitting? Did you stop by and chat with anyone? Do you recall what they were eating and drinking?"

She answered all the questions earnestly. I couldn't tell if there were any clues in her answers, as she was the first to submit. I thanked her for her cooperation and asked her to send the next person up when she returns to the general session room. As she opened the door to leave she said, "I hope you get to the bottom of this. It's not very flattering for the company."

I couldn't agree more, I thought. The next three people came and went. For some, it seemed that I had to wait longer than I anticipated for them to arrive for their appointment. While I waited, I wondered if they were dawdling in procrastination, or maybe taking extra time to rehearse their story. Perhaps they were so engrossed in a role-play that they needed extra time to finish before heading up to the interrogation room. I was beginning to run behind schedule and getting worried that I would not be able to finish by the lunch break.

Each individual interview was unique. And I learned a bit more about each one of them as they participated in this impromptu exercise — not personally or professionally — but I learned how they handle pressure, how they deal with perceived ambiguity, and the true nature of their fight or flight response. I didn't partake in small talk; there was no chit-chat as each "suspect" entered the suite. I was straight forward, matter of fact, and immediately launched into my line of questioning. This unnerved some of the individuals because my attitude and relationship with them so far, in my role as their learning leader, was far nicer, friendly, welcoming and approachable.

I got about three-quarters of the way through the interviews when the first of the Three Amigos entered the room. Jimmy sat down in the appointed spot, acting overly dumb-founded about the situation. He began each answer looking to the ceiling for inspiration, working hard to remember the specific details of his evening. I could not establish that he ate at the hotel restaurant; instead, he mentioned an off-site restaurant. It was funny that he could not remember the name of the place. It was also interesting to note that I had yet to interview the classmates with whom he had dinner. Jimmy was perhaps the first piece in the puzzle. When I asked him what he had for dinner, he responded quickly, saying, "a sandwich." "What kind of sandwich?" I asked. "Um, you know, just a regular sandwich … grilled with cheese and meat."

   "Was it a Monte Christo?" I asked.

"I don't recall the name of the sandwich. It was grilled with some meat and cheese. It came with French fries," he replied.

"Did anyone else order the same sandwich that you had, maybe ordering it to-go?"

"I don't think so. I don't recall anyone with a to-go bag, "he said.

I was thinking to myself, "I bet it's a Monte Christo." Jimmy seemed anxious to get out of the interrogation room. He asked me if that was all that I needed. When I gave him the green light, he bolted out of the room like bat out of hell.

Next up was Jason. He rapped on the suite door with the familiar tap-tap-ta-tap-tap … tap-tap. "Hello-hello," he announced. "Come in and sit down" I said, motioning to the empty chair across directly across the table.

"What's this I hear about Alison's room being charged with someone else's dinner?" he said.

I immediately launched into my line of questioning.
I don't didn't bother to pause to answer his question. I figure the questions I will be asking will speak for themselves. Jason seemed more interested than usual given his typically indifferent attitude. But, he managed to strike a balance between his interest in my line of questioning and being indignant at the thought of being the object of suspicion. He had an answer for each of my questions, albeit they were short. He did not embellish or look to the ceiling or out of the window for any answers. He did ponder the questions and think about his answer before giving it. It seemed as though he was prepared. It was as if he had prior knowledge of the questions and had rehearsed his answers.

Next up was Jeff. Jeff was obviously uncomfortable with the situation. If anyone looked and acted guilty, it was Jeff. Jeff was one of the Three Amigos. I thought it would be interesting to see how his story lined up with Jimmy's. I walked through the questions with Jeff and his story lined right up with Jimmy's. Both had dinner alone, both paid cash, both had a sandwich with fries. Both did not see anyone else from the class that night. Neither could remember the name of the restaurant where they ate; it was somewhere around the corner where all of the restaurants are located. Interesting. Given the fact that they are traveling on an expense report, they are required to turn in a receipt for anything spent over $25.00.

I find it rather convenient that out of all the interviews today, two spent cash on a dinner that did not exceed $25.00. How do you do that in this particular market? I supposed they ordered a sandwich platter that went for the going rate of $12 - $15 and ordered water only as a beverage. Not exactly how these guys roll. They struck me as burger and beer guys, at the very least.

I continued through the interrogations, noting the particulars. It was getting closer to lunch time, and I had three interviews left when the next person on the roster knocked on the door. I had to say, "Come in," even though the door was open and the person standing in the doorway could see me at the desk. That person was Matt. The last of the Three Amigos. He stopped in the doorway waiting for me to motion him all the way in to sit down. As he sat down, I looked up at him, but he did not make eye contact. Before I could get the first question out of my mouth, Matt blurted out, "I'm so sorry. I didn't want to do it, but they talked me into it."

"Do what?" I asked.

"Go along with the scam to use Allie's room number and name on our bill." He went on, "I told them that they would find out. I mean, who's going to let a bill for more than $400 get charged to the wrong room?"

"Okay, so tell me what happened, and start at the beginning," I asked. Matt took a deep breath and began his story.

"I went to work out with Jimmy and Jeff. We went to the gym, and afterwards we went to the putting greens golf course next door. We had a couple of beers and played nine holes. By the time we were done it was pretty dark, and we were starving. The putting green's restaurant was closing so we came back to the hotel. On our way in, we ran into Jason and Jodi. Jeff asked them if they wanted to join us, and they said that they already ate. Jimmy suggested that they come with us anyway and have a night cap. They both agreed, so the waitress seated us outside on the patio and gave us the menus. The first thing I noticed was that it was pricey. I didn't want to spend that kind of money for a dinner. Jimmy told me not to worry about it, and since the prices were so high, we might as well splurge and get the most expensive thing on the menu because anything less would not come close to the value. He said he would be able to get a discount. I asked how, and he said 'Don't worry about it, order the steak.' Jimmy, Jeff and I ordered the New York Strip with baked potato and Caesar salad. Jimmy ordered a round of Talisker Scotch, which he said is what James Bond always drinks. It was after 9:30 by the time we got dinner. We had a couple of more drinks, and Jimmy asked for the bill. When I asked what I owed, he told me not to worry about it, as he had a 'discount code.' Jason and Jodi finished their drinks, dropped $20 on the table and left after the waitress dropped off the check. I asked Jimmy where he got the discount code, and he started laughing. He turned the bill around so I could see it. He charged everything to Alison's room and forged her signature. He even bragged that he knows how to write 'real pretty.'"

I interrupted his story, "What about the sandwiches?"

"What sandwiches?" he replied.

"The Monte Christo sandwiches. There were six Monte Christos on the bill," I said, eagerly waiting for the sandwich story.

Matt had a puzzled look on his face. "Sandwiches?" he said to himself, looking up and around as if the answer was hidden somewhere in the room.

"Yes, sandwiches" I said. I took the bill out of my notebook and laid it on the table in front of him. "Does this ring a bell?"

"*Oh, those* Monte Christos!" Matt declared with surprise as he looked carefully at the bill. "I completely forgot about that. Those aren't sandwiches; those are cigars!"

So, there you have it. The mystery of the $25.00 sandwich wasn't a sandwich at all. It makes perfect sense that there are six on the bill. If you're going to commit fraud, you might as well go big and stock up!

So, did you guess who is the Monte Christo Lucifer? If you guessed Jimmy, you are spot on. The alpha male, the consummate entertainer, the savior-faire, debonair and his craving for power. His leadership translated into three terminations. When asked why he did it, he said, "Because I didn't think I would get caught."

What do we have here? We have fraud, theft and liars. Let's start with the liars. In my line of work, I've seen my share of liars. I knew that Alison was not lying when she approached me with her situation. Her authenticity gave her away. What was interesting was watching the body language of her colleagues throughout the interrogation process.

HOW TO SPOT A LIAR

In his article titled "How to Spot A Liar — By Analyzing His Body Language," John Alex Clark, points out the following Nonverbal Deception Cues:

> **Eye Direction:** *Research has shown that the eyes look to the left or right depending on whether they're lying or not. Looking up to the left means the person is using the creative part of their brain and are trying to imagine a picture of the story they are telling. Looking up to the right generally means they are remembering an actual image of an event and are just recounting that image to you in words. In essence, you can spot a liar in a high percentage of instances if they look up and to the left when telling their story.*

> **Hands:** *One way to spot a liar is to keep an eye on his hands, as liars have a tendency of hiding their palms. They are also unlikely to look you straight in the eye while lying or sit upright with a straight back.*

> **Story Inconsistencies:** *Another way to spot a liar is if their story changes over time. Events, times and dates changing will probably arouse your suspicion. However, don't make the common mistake of chalking such inaccuracies up to forgetfulness on their part. The simple equation is that the more lies you tell, the more you have to remember and in reality, the person is bound to forget lies they told you previously if they made them up on the spot.*

> **Confidence:** *Lack of confidence in their voice is one way to spot a liar. When a person lies they will naturally be less self-confident*

as they will fear you possibly finding out the truth. Peoples' voices tend to become lower too when lying, as well as slower. The liar might need to slow down his voice if they're literally making up the lies there and then in front of you. They will also come to more abrupt stops in their language as the subconscious scans to examine if what they're saying can be passed off as fact or is there is something in the story that could cause them to be found out.

Appearing Anxious: *Every liar will be anxious, but to what degree they show it will depend on their skill and experience of lying. When a person is anxious about a subject, they will want to move away from it as quickly as possible to another subject. If you want to increase their anxiousness, keep on talking about that subject to them and asking them questions about it. From there you can access more easily how much anxiety they are displaying.*

The body language was all there: Jimmy began each answer by looking to the ceiling for the answer, working hard to remember the specific details of his evening. Jason seemed more interested than usual, given his typically indifferent attitude. Sitting still on the edge of the chair, he answered questions swiftly and briefly. Matt was anxious and clearly acting guilty the minute he walked in and sat down. He caved before I got the first question out. Does this mean that Matt is truthful? Or is he a liar? Well, he ended up telling the truth, but his confession did not grant him a stay of execution. He was terminated for participating in the fraud. Yes, he questioned Jimmy when it happened, but became complicit when he turned a blind-eye. If only he had the integrity to stand up to Jimmy when he was committing the fraud! But he did not. Why? Because he was one of the Three Amigos. He was part of the "cool" guys. He belonged to a club with a powerful leader. He willingly engaged in illicit activity at the hand of Monte Christo Lucifer.

⇜ LUCIFER LESSON #1 ⇝
Conducting an Investigation

When conducting your investigation, be observant and note not just what they say, but *how* they say it! Don't keep your head buried in your notetaking; look up and take notice. Be respectful and ask questions with tact, and stick to the facts. While you don't want to come across as a prosecuting attorney, you also don't want to come across as flip or too congenial. You must maintain an appearance of seriousness and command.

> **When conducting your investigation, be observant and note not just what they say, but *how* they say it!**

Have a well-planned investigation. If HR cannot do the investigation, seek guidance from them on the dos and don'ts of the investigation and what you can and cannot ask. Organize the questions that you need to ask and remember to drill-down on ambiguous terms or information that needs a deeper understanding. For example, I asked Jimmy what he had for dinner, and he responded with "a sandwich." When I asked what type of sandwich, which is a *drill down* question, he couldn't recall, but he said it was "grilled with meat and cheese." I should have drilled down once more and should have asked, "What kind of meat?" I know what a Monte Christo sandwich is made of, so I may have missed a clue there.

Select the right location for your interviews. Make sure that it's confidential and secure, but don't promise complete confidentiality; after all, you will be reporting this to HR and to others in the organization who need to know. And above all, set your expectations so that you can maintain control of the interview. Professional investigators develop rapport with the person they are questioning to build trust. In this case, I had developed rapport and built trust over the past several days, so I set the expectation early on that this was serious, and that I had no time for small talk and chit chat.

⚡ LUCIFER LESSON #2 ⚡
Legit Leader or Lucifer?

A true leader does not need to entice followers with grand gestures or power plays.

Keep your eye on "the organizer:" the guy or gal who emerges as a magnet. They draw people toward them and collect them like pawns. They could be legit leaders, or they could be a Lucifer. So how do you know which is which? A true leader does not need to entice followers with grand gestures or power plays. The Lucifer Leader must be the center of attention and uses whatever it takes to rope their followers into becoming their disciples.

HIDDEN COSTS FROM MONTE CRISTO LUCIFER

When it was all said and done, in addition to losing three sales people with less than six months' tenure, we spent time and resources chasing down the truth: Translation — a significant amount of hidden cost from this Monte Cristo Lucifer Leader totaling $370,850!

CHAPTER SEVEN

Voyeur Lucifer

In today's world of advanced technological tools, information is traded, sent and posted at warp speed. The sales department is often the recipient of the best of what technology has to offer to do their job.

As technology evolves, so does the creativity of the end-user. I'm sure we've all heard stories of people using company equipment to run a side business, or play video games, or even surf for pornography. These examples moved a multitude of HR, Legal and IT departments to develop acceptable use policies for computing resources to mitigate the risk of damage to their companies and to their brand's reputation. But, can we put a price tag on such behavior? We can when it culminates into a risk that impacts many. The risk in this story cost the company plenty — $7 million. This is the story of Voyeur Lucifer.

All the sales people were provided with laptops to manage their day-to-day activities in their territories. Computer laptops are good for many things, and it certainly is not uncommon for a rep to use the device for personal use. It is understood that, from time to time, a rep may need to send an email to check on a child, set up a dental appointment, or to get directions to an event that is not sponsored or is located outside of the workplace. No harm, no foul, until we meet Voyeur Lucifer.

This Lucifer was hired into the organization from the competition. A quick-witted, dapper guy, he made friends quickly, and was always on the ever ready with a timely quip about the conversation *du jour*. His name was Wayne.

Wayne enjoyed selling and enjoyed the people he worked with. He was the kind of guy who had fun at work. He was very happy-go-lucky, and always seemed to be living life to its fullest. But, one thing that no one knew about Wayne was that he liked to take pictures of people when they were not looking. He was always snapping pictures of people in odd locations and poses. Most were strangers. He would even add some of his photos to his PowerPoint presentations during sales meetings. This would always make people in the meeting laugh with how he used the photos to get his point across.

The interesting thing about his photos, however, was that the face of the person was never visible. Wayne always took the picture from the side, or from behind, or from a special angle where there was something in the way of seeing the person's face. Without the face visible, the compromising position of the person being photographed seemed innocuous. But was it?

One day, Voyeur Lucifer made a joint sales call with Richard. Richard had met Wayne at an annual sales conference a few years back. They hit it off immediately; Wayne being the older and more experienced one, took Richard under his wing as his protégé. Richard affectionately called him "Dad." As they departed the building, Wayne snapped a photo of a woman coming back from lunch. The wind was blowing hard that day and was wreaking havoc on her pleated silk skirt. She had a difficult time keeping it from blowing up over her head like an umbrella turned inside-out in a storm. Her arms were flailing like an octopus grabbing at every direction the wind would blow. As she crossed the parking lot, head down and arms working, she rushed into the building.

When Wayne and Richard got into the car, Wayne took out his phone and began looking through the shots he had taken of the young lady crossing the parking lot. "BINGO!" Wayne exclaimed. "What is it?" responded Richard.

Wayne leaned over the passenger seat and showed Richard his prized shot. He managed to capture a moment in time where the woman's skirt had blown up enough to see all her undergarments. Her face was covered by her blowing hair, but the "under" shot was what he was looking for.

"Wow, she's got a great set of wheels," said Wayne. "Look how I got a perfectly clear shot; it almost looks as if you can feel the wind rustling around her."

"That's pretty cool," Richard replied. "But, isn't that a bit intrusive? You know; taking a picture of someone's intimates?"

"It's a photo without personal identity," said Wayne. "No one could ever identify who she is. Anyway, it's about the capture from the waist down."

"So, what do you do with these pictures, Wayne?" asked Richard.

"I created a website where I keep them organized," Wayne replied. "Do you want to see it?" he asked. "Sure," said Richard.

Wayne pulled up the website on his laptop using the hotspot feature on his mobile phone. He had them organized by the shot posed: breasts and buttocks, bending and leaning, public and private. He even had them sub-organized by race: African American, Latina, Asian, Caucasian, etc. Some were funny, but some were highly invasive and taken while the subject was in a restroom or locker room.

Richard was amazed at the breadth and depth of the collection. "How long have you been doing this?" Richard asked.

"I don't know, a couple of years or so," said Wayne. He went on, "Do you know what would be cool? We could have a contest and see who could get the best or most crazy pic!" Wayne said with excitement.

"What's in it for me, besides bragging rights?" asked Richard.

"Well, for starters, I'll set up a point system to qualify the shots. We can each contribute $5 a week into a kitty. Whoever posts a winning pic for the week, the other person throws in an extra $5 bucks. At the end of the month, whoever has the most points wins the pot."

"Ha! Love it! You're on!" exclaimed Richard.

And so, it began. Richard and Wayne embarked on their clandestine project, snapping all types of pictures. Richard started out as a novice. His photos were simple and mundane. It wasn't until he saw some of Wayne's recently posted pics that Richard got inspired.

It appears that Wayne somehow found his way into the ladies' restroom at a hotel. He parked himself in a stall, looking for his prey like a hyena lying in wait for the young wildebeest to innocently happen along.

Using a periscope rig he made from a telescoping hand mirror, he was able to get a view from the underside of the stall next to him without the mirror being detected. He then aimed his camera lens into the mirror. It was a perfect set up, from his twisted perspective. He disguised himself by wearing leggings underneath his work slacks, which he rolled up, and slipped on a pair of athletic shoes. From the outside, it looked like the person in the stall had just got out of an aerobics class. Disgustingly brilliant. He camped out there for quite some time, and ended up getting two "prized" bare-bottomed shots.

With his new-found inspiration, Richard boarded his flight to Houston. He took his usual window seat and looked around for any potential opportunities to one-up Wayne. His first opportunity arose when a woman stopped at his row and began loading her luggage into the overhead bin. Her shirt was untucked and hemmed at her mid-drift. Richard leaned over toward the aisle with his phone in hand, acting as if he had dropped something under the center seat. He snapped the picture; sure enough, he got the bra shot while the woman was arranging her luggage. His luck was extended when a second female passenger entered his row, taking the center seat. As she was getting adjusted, she leaned forward to place her purse under the seat in front of her. She had to lean at an angle to get the bag stuffed into the compartment. In so doing, she twisted her body toward Richard, using her right hand to slide the bag under the seat. Her shirt was a scoop neck, jersey knit that stretched tight across her bustline as she leaned into the reach.

Meanwhile, Richard had to lean back and stand up slightly in the window seat to give the woman the room she needed to get her bag under the seat. As he made the adjustment, he pretended to be intensely reading his email, when in fact, he was jockeying for an aerial shot of the cleavage below. With a silent tap of a button, he was able to get the shot without missing a beat. He wanted to look at the pictures so badly, but was afraid that someone behind him might see what he was doing. So, he decided to wait until he could look at them without risk.

The flight took off and made it to its destination without incident. Richard could hardly wait to get into the taxi to look at his photographic work. He really wanted to win the weekly contest. He navigated his way throughout the airport and out to the transportation staging area where he got in line for his taxi. As soon as he got inside the car, he pulled out his phone. He immediately went to the collection of pictures he took on the plane. Wow, they were good, really good, he thought. Richard had some prized shots, and best of all, you could not tell that they were taken on an airplane. They were close-ups, with great angles, and no face. For sure he thought he had a winner.

Once he reached his destination, he met up with one of his colleagues, Anthony. Anthony was a local rep who had known Richard for a couple of years. They had become pretty close over time and seemed to cut it up a lot when they were together; they were always laughing and joking around. They met at the hotel bar where Richard was staying and ordered a round of drinks while they started to catch up.

Anthony began to tell Richard about an incident that happened when he was on a customer site visit. As Anthony described it, his customer has a glass-enclosed conference room in the front lobby across from the reception area restrooms. While he was in the conference room with his customer, a gentleman exited the men's room with his shirt tail tucked neatly into and out through the zipper of his fly, and didn't even know it. The starch in the shirt tail created a silhouette that screamed "full salute!" The visual alone made both of them roar with laughter.

"You should have gotten a picture of that," said Richard.

"Ha! How was I going to that, dumbass? Tell my customer, wait a sec, I've got a get a picture of your boss's stub chub?" replied Anthony.

"Too bad you were with your customer. That would have been a money shot," said Richard. "What do you mean?" said Anthony.

"Wayne started a little club where we post pictures that we take of people in compromising positions, and we post them to a private website that he created. We each chip in $5 every week. Whoever has the best pic wins the pot," said Richard. He went on to show Anthony the two shots that he got on the flight.

"Check these out. I think either one can win," Richard exclaimed. He showed Anthony the pictures, much to his friend's amazement.

"Ha! Those are awesome. I see photo ops all the time and think to myself, *Wow, that would be quite a shot!* Can I get into the club?" asked Anthony.

"I don't see why not. Let me ping Wayne," Richard replied. And before they were called for their dinner reservation, Anthony was in the club too.

As the weeks went on, Anthony, Richard and Wayne recruited two women and three more men to join the group. They were all part of a clique that was formed long ago at an internal sales conference. By then they had $40 in the pool every week and the competition was hot. Each week the club members posted their photos. They posted pictures of males, females, and even animals in compromising situations. And, if the pictures weren't bad enough, they started posting jokes; off-color jokes, ethnic jokes and jokes with racial overtones. It was a frenzy.

It didn't take long before "the club" became a major distraction and a disruption in the sales productivity of each of the participants. They spent more time following jokes, stalking co-workers and strangers for "the money shot," and loading their pirate booty up to Wayne's website.

It was all fun and games until Wayne had a little set back. For some reason, Wayne's laptop started to act up. First, it was slow, and then it was sticky slow, and finally, he got the "blue screen of death." The only thing he could do was to send the laptop to IT for diagnosis and repair. He put in his ticket and sent the laptop to the corporate office. He was pissed, not because it set him back with his proposals, presentations and access to important sales files, but because it would make it very difficult for him to keep up with the others in the weekly contest. Wayne didn't have a computer at home, so it would be a hassle for him to keep up with his daily posts. Wayne hated to lose. He was highly competitive, and as the ring leader and originator of the website, he did not want to fall behind.

Meanwhile, the IT department began their work on Wayne's computer. As they peeled back the layers of code and history, they came across some surprising content. The IT person working on the laptop called another one over to look: "Check this out," he said to his colleague. The colleague looked at the screen and reacted with surprise. As the two continued to peer into the screen, other IT professionals gathered around the screen, looking on in awe. With mouths hanging open and eyes wide with amazement, there was a silence so still that you'd think that someone had just died.

Yes, it was the bomb that Wayne left on his computer, one so vola-
tile that the device seemed to smoke as the IT professionals clicked
through the images. Each picture was more horrendous than the
other, so much so that all the onlookers took a step backward simultaneously as if they would become contaminated by an airborne pixel
particle emanating from the screen.

The jig was up. HR was alerted to the secret website. There was
a tower of evidence. The evidence was as strong as steel. Each
webpage reflected the demoralizing behavior that stood behind it.
It was amazing how much of the site was built using other people to
crowd-source the content.

HR uncovered it all; the jokes, the emails, the compromising pictures,
and the book-makers' tally of money collected, pay outs, dispersion
schedule and more.

All the evidence made it an epic year for Wayne, but not in a good
way. Every conceivable image that he brought to the company
equipment was now documented and filed as evidence of IT
"non-compliance."

As the investigation continued, HR uncovered Richard's connection
to Wayne along with the slew of pictures he posted. The discovery
of Richard's participation led to the unmasking of Anthony, which
led to the trail of racial jokes posted by Shelia and Karin, which in
turn fingered Darnell and Jackson with their ridiculous escalation of
everything. The scope of the participation was monumental. It not
only violated the company's anti-harassment and anti-sexual harassment policies, it burned right through the code of conduct policy that
was the cornerstone of the company's coveted award ranking it as
one of the Best Places to Work.

ABILITY TO INFLUENCE

> He had a strong ability to influence those who have aspirations of being a "player," a "top dog," and part of the "inner circle."

How was it that Wayne was able to recruit and train his fellow colleagues to engage in such illicit behavior? He was a Lucifer Leader. He had a strong ability to influence those who have aspirations of being a "player," a "top dog," and part of the "inner circle." Wayne knew who they were. He pegged their personalities like a forensic psychologist profiling their criminal mark. Let us not forget that Richard called Wayne, "Dad." He looked up to him and trusted him. He wanted to please him in an effort to gain and keep his attention. By garnering Wayne's affection, Richard could validate his position as a valued member of the team. Through his recruitment of Anthony, Richard elevated his position to that of a lieutenant. As the group grew, so did the importance of every preceding member.

⚞ LUCIFER LESSON #1 ⚟
Camaraderie versus Clique

> There is a difference between camaraderie on the team and a "clique" on the team.

There is a difference between camaraderie on the team and a "clique" on the team. Camaraderie is a wonderfully normal way that groups of people who spend a lot of time together share mutual trust and friendship. Cliques, on the other hand, represent an elite group that considers themselves better than the rest of collective relationships in the organization. They are damaging on many levels: First, they alienate other team members. Second, they are secretive and covert with their interactions and communications. Have you ever witnessed the secret handshake? The "high-five" with an added move? These are the actions that physically set the clique apart from the rest. So, if you witness the formulation of a clique, permeate and break it up. Double-down on your own leadership skills and make the environment inclusive for everyone. Maybe, along the way, you might get tipped-off about the actions of the clique.

⫸ LUCIFER LESSON #2 ⫷
Look for Pockets of Discontent

Lucifer Leaders are like a virus. They can corrupt good people on your team.

Lucifer Leaders are like a virus. They can corrupt good people on your team. The Voyeur Lucifer wasn't exactly secret with his conquests. After all, he used his intrusive photos from time to time in his PowerPoint decks that he presented to the sales team during sales meetings. Sure, the photos made people laugh, but why was it condoned? By allowing this to continue, it became the very catalyst that influenced the others' inner compasses and transformed them into pursing behavior they would not normally partake in. All the signs were there: the photos, the off-color jokes in the sales meetings, the clique. So, when you see something that is off-color, somewhat indecent or in poor taste, put a stop to it and investigate. Nip it in the bud early before the virus spreads.

❧ LUCIFER LESSON #3 ❧
Create a Transparent Culture

Considering the #MeToo movement, you don't want to wind up on the front page of anything. In addition to sexual harassment training, go beyond and educate your employees on how to create a transparent culture that does not tolerate racism, sexism, bullying or counter-productive workplace behavior. Implement periodic "temperature checks" on employee engagement and look for pockets of discontent. Train champions in the workforce to stop bad behavior when it occurs. It's a long road, but together, we can greatly reduce this type of behavior in the workforce.

HIDDEN COSTS FROM VOYEUR LUCIFER

At the end of the investigation, eight people were accused. Of the eight accused, five were fired. The terminations represented a good deal of monthly revenue generation. And, with the elimination of these five producers, the lost opportunity cost was staggering.

The cost of this Lucifer Leader was huge. These individuals were all well-performing sales reps. They had varying degrees of tenure with the company, but what they all had in common was their thirst for competition. They exhibited the thrill of the chase and a thirst for the win. Five performers selling at an annual pace of $1.13 million per year equaled $5.65 million. That's a hard pill to swallow.

Sure, the organization has a pipeline, and other reps can be assigned to the accounts in their pipeline, but how much of that can we realistically capture and close? According to *Salesforce Blog*, 6% of opportunities are converted to sales, but that's considering that the opportunities are being worked. Enter a termination: How long does it take for the sales manager to assign the prospects to a different sales rep on the team? The rep that gets the assignment has his/her own pipeline to work. What are the odds that they are going to sift through all the opportunities (and corresponding notes) in the terminated sales rep's CRM to find the gold? The long shot is a capture rate of .01% of the terminated rep's pipeline, if you are that lucky.

Let's talk hidden costs. Terminating five members of the sales team will make some waves with the rest of the team members. What will their distraction cost be? They will undoubtedly talk about the situation among themselves and with their friends and families, and maybe with some unsuspecting potential customers. What is that going to cost? And what about the repercussions from the victims? Is it possible that the photos could leak outside of the company? How long does the company have to carry the burden of the bad deeds, wondering when the other shoe will drop. Wow. This presents a nightmare of epic proportions.

DOWNSTREAM RAMIFICATIONS OF DEVIANT BEHAVIOR

Finally, let's add a SUPER hidden cost. I call this SUPER because no one ever thinks about the downstream ramifications of deviant behavior: The cost to roll out training to everyone in the organization on code of conduct, harassment, sexual harassment, and internet technology acceptable use policies. Hopefully you have these trainings in place already and a system of delivering it annually. If you do, think about the soft cost to make that happen: communications, pushing out the training, following up to make sure everyone completed it, the time the organization needs to complete the training, and the lost sales productivity associated with it.

If you don't have this training in place, add the cost to curate the training and ready it for deployment! You can purchase a course off-the-shelf for a few hundred dollars, but you must have someone qualified to teach it. If it is an instructor-led course, this might set you back $1,500 per session. If you purchase an e-Learning course online, you might spend anywhere from a few hundred bucks for a generic program and up to $30,000 for a highly-customized version. Then, you must deliver it — a.k.a., a learning management system, which runs anywhere from $5,000 per year to hundreds of thousands of dollars per year depending on the number of employees you have. Add this up and that's a whopper of a number! That's a hidden cost that few account for.

This Lucifer, and his impact, had devastating consequences. $7 million dollars can put many companies out of business, or at the very least, set them back months behind achieving their numbers. If you are a public company, how do you position that type of guidance to Wall Street? Businesses cannot afford a backward-looking strategy. They need to be pro-active.

Benjamin Franklin once said, "If you fail to plan, you are planning to fail!" What if we were more cognizant of the potential for deviant behavior and planned ahead to mitigate the cost associated with it, using forward thinking, rather than trying to manage it after the fact? The investment in the establishment of solid compliance policies and good quality awareness training can mean the difference between $100,000 and $7 million!

Whether you are a sales manager, sales trainer, or HR practitioner, you know that when budget cuts need to be made, the first cut in the budget is training. Training is cut because we don't create training that addresses business outcomes and we don't measure trainings return on investment. If we want a seat at the table, we have to serve up a dish that's palatable by our stakeholders. This story is a perfect case study with which to create a business case for an argument that the investment is worth the expense.

CHAPTER EIGHT

Imperious Lucifer

As the old expression goes, "the fish stinks from the head." Meaning, that if the subordinate is behaving badly, it's because of the manager. Many Lucifers are spawned by the leaders that they follow. In the case of Imperious Lucifer, this "fish" directly and indirectly cost the company $4,350,000 in legal fees, and lost opportunities..

If the subordinate is behaving badly, it's because of the manager. Many Lucifers are spawned by the leaders that they follow.

It began as it usually does, with an opening for a Vice President of Sales. The recruiter was told to seek candidates who were hard drivers and able to turn around poor performing teams. They wanted candidates with backbone who would not stand down when challenged. So, the recruiters began their search and paraded candidate after candidate to the powers that be. At last, they settled on an individual who worked for the competition. He was extremely confident, and quickly rose up through the ranks at his former job, leap-frogging roles and hop-scotching across the country to executive-level glory.

His interviewing skills were impressive. He had a silver tongue, dripping with sales operational speak and multiple stories about his pinnacle conquests. He was the Messiah they were looking for: YOU'RE HIRED!

His employment began as most executive-level positions do; there is no established or official onboarding program. Instead, the newly-minted VP enjoys several one-on-one meetings with other executives and a week's-worth of lunches. Along the way, he learns that sales have been off for ten months in a row. The sales pipeline was weak, and the sales managers were often missing their forecasts.

His conversation with the Chief Financial Officer sounded as if the sales people were order takers and not "consultative enough." According to the CFO, the sales people were leaving too much margin on the table or discounting at the command of the customer without so much as an effort to overcome price objections.

His conversation with the Chief Human Resources Officer exposed a mature sales force that was likely set in their ways, and perhaps, not properly linking their sales process with the changing customer buying process. Turnover was low, and for any of the sales professionals that did exit the organization, their exit interviews shared a common theme around compensation. It appeared that the compensation might not be aligned with the organization's strategy. Maybe the sales folks weren't focused on the right activities because of their compensation plan.

The Chief Information Technology Officer talked at length about the CRM tool, and how poorly the data input was managed. There were no standards set for how the sales people entered information, coded stages of the sales, or reported wins and losses. To the CIO, the customer relationship management tool was a waste of time and money, and it would take a yeoman's effort to get the data shored up for it to be of any use at all.

The interview with the Vice President of Marketing took a journey through the many campaigns over the last three years, along with the results of the voice of the customer for each of the campaigns that her team rolled out. It was an interesting conversation as the VP of Sales learned that, while customers liked the product releases, they were not as pleased with the purchase options — there weren't enough ways for the customer to take delivery, and the billing options were very limited.

The CEO had his own view from the Bridge. He genuinely liked the sales people. He looked at them as honest and trustworthy professionals who had the customers' best interests at heart. According to the CEO, the sales people need a little TLC, direction and sales leadership. He's done what he could do insofar as paying for some skills training, and adding a few spiffs here and there. The former VP of Sales was with the company for 35 years and retired 10 months ago. It had taken the company this long to find the right person. The CEO really needed to turn this sales department around, and he believed that a fresh vision would motivate and invigorate the team.

After a week of interviews, the new VP of Sales concluded to himself that the CEO was weak, the VP of Marketing was clueless, the CIO didn't know a thing about CRM's, and the CHRO and CFO should spend more time on their respective roles and do more to support sales. With this as his backdrop, the VP of Sales set out to the field to meet with the sales managers and the sales people.

In his first regional sales meeting, he opened with a line that came straight out of *Glengarry Glen Ross*, and he wasn't joking: "Welcome to a new dawn in sales for this company," he said, and added, "Sales have been off for 10 straight months and it's going to stop now." He continued with, "Not meeting your numbers is no longer acceptable." There was dead silence. The sales managers looked stunned as the sales reps looked down at their notebooks, not making eye-contact with anyone in the room. "I'm going to establish standards for how you manage your day and increase the amount of time you spend with prospects and customers." The VP announced, "We will become efficient and productive."

The VP went on with his presentation, jotting down numbers on a flip chart, and sprinkling his speech with the results he achieved with the competition. He came across as a ball-buster as the winds of change blew a chill into the room. When the meeting was over, the VP asked the sales managers to stay while the rank-and-file exited the room in silence. As soon as they got out of earshot from the VP, the buzz picked up. They obviously were not happy campers. Some talked of getting their resumes ready, and others wanted to seek revenge. There weren't many who felt like stepping up to the plate. The meeting was less than motivational.

Meanwhile, the sales managers got an ear-full. "You're a bunch of desk jockeys," the VP shouted. "You're complacent and behind your peers at other companies when it comes to the execution of sales activities. You can't hit a forecast if it stared you right in the face," he lamented. "It's going to stop and it's going to stop now." He then preceded to lay out the plan for the sales managers. They learned that they will be riding with their sales reps four out of five days. On the first Monday of each week, they will have one-on-one meetings with each rep and review all active prospects and accounts in the pipeline. They would determine the viability of each proposal using a pre-set criterion. If the account did not meet the specific criteria, it would be coded as a dead deal and taken out of the pipeline. If it was determined that there was something that the corporate office could do to support the potential sale, the manager needed to report it to the VP of Sales on their weekly round-table review. If the numbers were not trending up in 30 days, the sales manager would be put on a performance improvement plan. If the numbers continued to lag, the manager would be terminated after 60 days.

By the time the new VP of Sales left the meeting, the entire population of sales managers and sales reps across the country heard about the new rules, and the "New Guy." They dreaded the coming attraction and loathed the idea of this guy going out to see customers. He mentioned in the meeting that he would be riding with reps in the field to get an idea of their skill levels and what he was dealing with. He needed to know how much turnover he would need to be prepared for.

As word spread like wild fire across the organization, the CEO got a phone call from one of the managers giving him a head's up that everyone will eventually be fired in the next 60 days, and the beatings will continue until there is improvement. The CEO was taken aback by this conversation and called the VP of Sales to discuss what he had heard.

Over the phone, the VP of Sales reminded the CEO that he was hired to turn around a poor performing sales force, and that the company wanted a head-strong, no-nonsense leader who would not accept losing excuses. "You have to beat them over the head to get their attention," the VP said. He added, "Don't worry, you will see improvement within the next 30 days, I promise; I know what I'm doing." The CEO politely asked that he tone down the rhetoric a bit as he continued to meet with the rest of the sales team. "Not a snowball's chance in hell," the VP replied. "Like a drill sergeant, I will get them to where they need to be, just as you hired me to do." He added, "I've done it before and I will do it again." The CEO sternly replied, "I do not want to see a mass exodus on my hands." The VP told him not to worry, "Once they start closing deals, they will be happy and won't want to leave, and it's going to happen quickly."

The CEO wasn't sure about the "voodoo" that this VP insisted will magically turn the sales force around, but he was watching.

Within the first two weeks of the new regime, the pipeline lost half of its original opportunities. This was not a good sign for sales managers who didn't want to be put on a performance improvement plan. There's no way that they will be able to make up the deficit in two weeks' time, so they knew that things were going to start to get ugly.

Meanwhile, Imperious Lucifer set out to accompany various sales reps in the field. He wanted to learn, first hand, what his sales force was made of. Each time he set up a scheduled field ride, he drilled the rep on where they are going and why they are going there. If there aren't enough appointments set for the day, the VP gave the rep the names of companies in his/her territory to cold call. Interestingly, it is these extra cold calls that seemed to be the "mojo" that the team needed. On each of these calls, the VP has the magic touch with the specific value proposition that resonated with the customer. He knew the exact questions to ask to learn where the sales rep can position an attractive option. And, most of all, he had the magic touch when it came to price. It was uncanny; wherever he directed the rep to go, they submitted a proposal and the close ratio was high for these types of accounts.

Word started to get around that this guy had the "secret sauce" to make things happen, but it wasn't good enough for Imperious Lucifer, and the beatings continued. He set up weekly meetings with the sales managers, berating them on their sales postings and the pipeline results of the first two weeks of one-on-ones. He put several sales managers on performance improvement plans.

The pressure trickled down to the sales reps. They were all feeling the heat and were becoming more and more desperate each day. Imperious Lucifer was particularly hard on a sales rep named Aaron. He rode with him often and hijacked the selected cold calls that he ordered Aaron to schedule. And then, during the monthly region call, he cited his conquests to humiliate Aaron in front of his peers. Aaron went to his sales manager for help, but the sales manager told him to not rock the boat. "Do you want to lose your job?" the sales manager opined. "He's got an ego the size of Texas, and he is obviously a narcissist. Don't let him get to you," he added.

It took everything that Aaron had to stand down and not rock the boat. It ate at him every day. He could not get the sound of Imperious Lucifer's voice out of his head. It consumed him on a daily basis, and he began to fantasize about how he could seek revenge.

As time marched on, Imperious Lucifer continued down his autocratic course, beating his chest and spraying his scent across the country.

During a scheduled field ride with a rep named Brent, whose territory was close to the corporate office, Imperious Lucifer left a green bar print-out in the back seat of Brent's car. At the end of the day, Brent dropped Imperious Lucifer back at the corporate office and headed out for the bar to meet up with Marco, a fellow sales rep. After he parked the car, he glanced back and saw a pile of green-bar paper in his back seat. It must belong to "Dickhead," he thought. He picked it up, looked it over, and decided to bring it into the bar with him to take a closer look. Brent walked in and looked over at the people sitting at the bar, searching for his buddy. Marco saw him at the front door and waved him over to the corner end of the bar.

"What's the five-pound anchor you're hauling around?" Marco asked. "It's a print out that "Dickhead" left on my back seat today," Brent replied. What is it?" asked Marco.

"I'm not sure, but it looks like a list of companies with information about the products they are supplied and the price they are paying," said Brent. He added, "I don't recognize any of the accounts on the list as existing customers." "Let me see it," said Marco, as he grabbed the 14" X 11" slab of dot-matrix-printed paper out of the hands of his friend.

Marco looked it over thoroughly, and along the way, pointed out a couple of accounts that he recently cold-called when Imperious Lucifer was riding with him. "Here's an account that Dickhead made me call on when he rode with me last week." He continued, "he quoted the guy on the spot and we closed the sale. It wasn't big, but it was nice to add something to the 'win' column."

"Let me look at that," Brent said. And he began flipping through the alphabetical listings, running his finger down the list until it rested on a specific account, he said, "Hey, check this out, this is an account we visited today!"

The two reps continued looking through the green-bar stack, analyzing the content and concluding that it is a customer list from the competitor. It was the same competitor that Imperious Lucifer came from.

"Wow, this is fantastic," said Brent.

"Are you thinking what I'm thinking?" said Marco?

And together they decided that this was a gift from God, and their "find" would be their salvation from being terrorized by the VP of

Sales, their Imperious Lucifer. They decided to make a copy of the book, and put the original copy back in Brent's car.

When Imperious Lucifer asked about it the next day, Brent retrieved the papers from his back seat and brought it to him as if he had given it no thought.

The green-bar sheet started turning positive right away. They had the "Glengarry Glen Ross" leads. Easy pickings. All they needed to do was find the accounts in their respective zip codes and start calling on them. Each account included the company name, address, phone number, principle decision maker, billing cycle, contract expiration date, product type and quantity, and price. They decided to create a campaign, approaching each of the accounts with an offer to save the prospect some money — correction— a *lot* of money to make a switch.

Both reps' pipelines started filling up, with each account qualified to perfection. They could literally watch the opportunities work their way through each stage of the funnel. They became somewhat of celebrities at the office. Their sales manager was happy because their performance took the spotlight off the office, giving the manger some breathing room.

Brent and Marco continued to peel through the green bar accounts, enjoying an 80% close ratio on a 45-day sales cycle. Their winning ways freed up some of their time to pursue other activities, such as golf. It was during one such golf outing that Marco got a message from his sales manager urging him to call right away. It turned out that the competitor, whose accounts Brent and Marco were pursuing, started litigation against the company for poaching their customers. They were being accused of Tortious Interference, and the competitor had substantial evidence to prove it.

"What the hell is Tortious Interference?" Brent asked.

"I have no idea, and what does it have to do with us?" Marco responded.

Marco and Brent collected themselves and headed back to the office to meet with their sales manager. On the drive back, they tried to imagine what the situation was about and what the impact to them might be.

"Maybe it's some stupid formality that we have to sign off on or something," Brent said.

"I don't know," said Marco. "I have a feeling that it's not going to be good."

When they got back to the office, the two entered the sales manager's office and took the two seats directly across from his desk.

"I'm not going to sugar coat this, but the two of you are in some pretty deep trouble," he said. He continued, "We have been contacted by the competitor's attorneys and have been subpoenaed by a judge to turn over records and contracts for every sale that you've made over the last six months."

"Why?" said Brent.

"Because someone has been poaching the accounts from our competitors, using an illegally obtained customer list and by undercutting the price they are paying." He went on to say, "A majority of the accounts that you and Marco sold came from the list."

"It sounds serious, " Marco said.

"Yes, it is," the manager responded.

The sales manager went on to explain that someone called the legal department at the competitor's corporate office and told them that he saw first-hand that one of their customer lists was given to us and we were using it to specifically target their accounts.

It turned out that Aaron had made the call to the legal department. He did so, not to punish Brent and Marco, he did it to rat out Imperious Lucifer and bury him like the pile of dog crap that he was. The investigation ensued, and the legal teams were assembled. The depositions went on and on, and the fees ratcheted up. After more than 24 months of investigation and legal wrangling, Marco and Brent were terminated, as was Aaron. But, Imperious Lucifer survived. He was able to keep his job and eventually rise to the rank of Senior Vice President.

A leopard never changes his spots. With the tortious interference behind him, Imperious Lucifer needed to ramp up the revenue chase. He became more and more cocky every day, taking on the marketing department, the training department, and the recruiting process from HR; one by one he stacked the deck to increase his power base. And, he spent money along the way. Too much money.

His efforts did not improve results, so he soon began increasing the sales goals. The targets were set high and difficult for the sales people to attain. It didn't take long for Imperious Lucifer to be forced to cover his tracks to make himself look good during the executive operations reviews. He started misrepresenting the numbers using a method of pipeline smoke and mirrors. With every subsequent review it became more and more difficult for him to save face. He was finally called on his bullshit. The CEO could listen no longer to the lies and fired him during the middle of an operating review.

Poetic justice served the sales organization that day for having to endure Imperious Lucifer's leadership over a period of three years.

⟫⟫ LUCIFER LESSON #1 ⟪⟪
Beware of the Shiny Object

When it sounds too good to be true, it probably is.

Beware of the shiny object! When it sounds too good to be true, it probably is. Have you ever hired anyone who you thought was 'da bomb' who turned out to be a dud? It's hard for hiring managers who are not intimate with the sales leader function to get it right when it comes to hiring an executive sales leader. You want confidence, you want a modicum of bravado and you want a track record. Think about the CEO with a finance background interviewing and evaluating the efficacy of a sales executive; sure, he can evaluate business acumen and a lot of other variables, but sales has such a mystique to it. Can an over-the-top narcissist blind the CEO's evaluation skills? Imperious Lucifer was a narcissistic leader. He has two sides; the first is fueled by his ego. It's the source of his energy. The second is his sociopathic underpinnings. The narcissist, in this case, fails to see his vulnerabilities and made the environment uncomfortable. He lacks awareness of his destructive behavior even when direct feedback is delivered to him. The sociopath side of Imperious Lucifer possesses no empathy; he gets bored easily if he is not constantly stirring the pot, which disrupts the organization in a bad way. If it looks too good to be true, dig before you say, "I do!"

⟫🔥 LUCIFER LESSON #2 🔥⟪
Personality Slips

Keep an eye open for personality slips. We saw some glimpses into Imperious' narcissistic personality disorder: His arrogance and failure to recognize the CEO's feelings about the sales force. His bravado in the way he addressed the sales managers for the first time. These signs were visible early on. They resurfaced often and culminated in the grandiose gestures he made to cover his lack of performance. On the flip side, he lacked the epitome of a good leader at every turn. He implemented solutions quickly without gaining buy-in or asking for feedback. He didn't listen to people, and he ordered them around. He always acted as if he was smarter than the rest. He was always right.

⟫🔥 LUCIFER LESSON #3 🔥⟪
Performance Management Practices

Establish expectations, align goals, and provide feedback. Revisit this often. If things are not moving in the right direction, take action before it's too late.

Don't be afraid to deliver frank feedback to a Lucifer and engage in good performance management practices no matter what level the person holds in the organization. Stage an intervention if you must. The earlier you get it out on the table the better. Establish expectations, align goals, and provide feedback. Revisit this often. If things are not moving in the right direction, take action before it's too late.

For years, it has not been uncommon for companies to turn a blind eye to performance issues when the perpetrator is a producer. Worse, they become especially sheepish when it's an executive. We've all seen it. I don't have to cite additional examples.

⇥🔥 LUCIFER LESSON #4 🔥⇤
Time Will Tell

The fish stinks from the head. *The Phrase Finder* defines this ages-old saying as: "When an organization or state fails, it is the leadership that is the root cause."[1] In the case of Brent and Marco, they engaged in deviant behavior based on the actions of their leader. Imperious Lucifer led them to the trap by virtue of his actions.

HIDDEN COSTS FROM IMPERIOUS LUCIFER

What are the hidden costs? While the litigation was pending, Imperious Lucifer had his hands full and spent a lot of money to take care of duties that he should have been doing on his own, in his own role. The cost for additional head count, and software licenses and training he spent to be able to perform his job while he was distracted with the litigation cost the company $850,000 over a two-year period.

Three unsuspecting sales people, who were trapped in the snare of Imperious Lucifer were terminated at a cost of $3,200,000 in salary, lost opportunity, and customer defection. Tragic that the sales reps got stuck holding the bag. They were led to their actions by fear

---

1   *The Phrase Finder*, founded in 1997 by Gary Martin. www.phrases.org.uk.

— fear of losing their jobs. They fell victim to the Lucifer Leader. The icing on the cake are the legal fees and expenses incurred by the company for the defense of Imperious Lucifer and the pending judgements were $300,000. All told, this Lucifer cost the company a bundle and worse, cost several people their jobs.

In the end, a narcissistic leader is toxic, and this becomes readily apparent over time. In an interview by Matt Staggs, Dr. Stanton Samenow, a clinical psychologist, said, "The three most frequent words I use in working with criminals are: time will tell."[2]

---

2   *Forbidden Fruits: A Journey Inside the Criminal Mind* with Dr. Samenow, by Matt Staggs, September 10, 2014, signature-reads.com.

CHAPTER NINE

Wardrobing Lucifer

I'm going to finish my exposé on Lucifer Leaders with one last story. It's a short one. This Lucifer did not cost the company hundreds of thousands of dollars, but he terminated quickly, within a month of his return from sales training. So, from a cost standpoint, he was a bad hire and cost the company time and money recruiting, hiring and training for what turned out to be an eventual downfall. This is the story of Wardrobing Lucifer.

The week-long sales training event kicked off with its usual parlance. We began with introductions, explored our thoughts about selling and training and then jumped in. We had a diverse group who seemed lively and engaged. After the first 90 minutes, we took a short break. I mingled with the group, getting to know the attendees better and developing rapport along the way. As I turned to grab a cup of coffee, I caught a glimpse of Eugene out of the corner of my eye. Eugene was an older gentleman, the most senior of the cohort. The objective he set for his week in sales training was "to teach an old dog new tricks." He was the only attendee who came to the meeting dressed in a full-on business suit, even though the invitations stated business casual. It was a nice suit, too. Expensive looking. I did a double-take because I noticed that he had a price tag securely attached to his rear-end.

I debated with myself, in silence, whether to point it out to him. Because he was the only person in the room, I decided to tell him.

"Hey, Eugene," I called out to him. "You have a tag attached to the back side of your slacks, I thought you'd like to know."

"Oh, thanks for letting me know," he replied.

"I have scissors in the box on the materials table. Help yourself," I said.

"Great! I appreciate that!" he said.

So, I grabbed my cup of coffee and became distracted with another attendee who had walked back into the room. Soon, the break was over, and it was time to get back to business. As the course of the day went on, I could not help but notice that Eugene never removed the tag on the seat of his pants. Instead, he tucked it into the slacks' back pocket. I guess he didn't have time, or maybe he was waiting to get back to the hotel to remove it. I know firsthand what can happen to an expensive pair of slacks when you try to cut something off while twisting backward and looking into a mirror! Chances are, I'm going to slice right through a piece of fabric!

We finished the day and sent the attendees back to the hotel. I organized the general session room for the next day and called it a night.

Day-two rolled around, and everyone was on time, bright-eyed and bushy-tailed. We serve a full breakfast at the training center, so it's nice to have the time for the attendees to socialize and get into the groove. I actually liked this time of day because I get to hear about the stories from the night before; who did what, where did they go, what did they explore, etc. At least Eugene was dressed a little more casually than yesterday. Gosh, he's so GQ! For a senior gentleman, he sure knows how to dress. He showed up in gabardine slacks, with a crisp and neatly pressed button-down shirt and a bright red cashmere sweater tied around his shoulders like a preppy ivy-league freshman. Ha! So tidy!

The morning went according to plan; lunch was great, and the afternoon was humming along. At the break, I noticed what looked like a horn or a blade underneath Eugene's sweater, like a kick-stand on his back. This time I didn't hesitate.

"Hey, Eugene, there's something under your sweater, on your back, it's sticking up," I said, pointing to my own shoulder blade as if I had the same thing going on.

Eugene looked over his shoulder and untied the sweater from his neck. "Ha, it's the tag," he said, as if he's amused.

"Did you buy all new outfits for training this week, Eugene?" I asked with an approving smile.

"I got a few things," he responded (with a wink and a nod).

The attendees reconvened, and we finished out day two uneventfully. Same drill as day one, everyone headed back to the hotel, had dinner on their own, and then were back at the training center for day three.

It is on this day, day three of a five-day session, when I was floored. Eugene entered the general session room wearing khaki pants with an awesome belt and loafers to match. His black long-sleeved polo shirt was tucked-in neatly. He dropped his bag (which has a tag on it) and turned toward the coffee carafe. It's at that very moment that I saw a price tag attached firmly to the cuff of his polo shirt. It can't be. Could it? I mean, it's been *three days of price tags*!

> "Eugene, why are you still coming to class with clothes that still have the price tags on?" I blurted out (from the surprise of addressing it three days in a row).

> "I'm returning all of these clothes to the store when I get back to Florida," he said plainly.

"Wow, did I just hear that?" I thought. Let's process that for a minute: Is this deviant behavior? Is it ethical deviance or integrity deviance? There is a difference. According to DifferenceBetween.com (posted January 13, 2015, by admin): *"The concepts of ethics and integrity go in a similar line yet have a clear difference between the two. These two words are specifically emphasized in organizational settings. When speaking of ethics, in all professions there are ethics. People stand by these ethics as a manner of avoiding any dilemmas. Integrity, on the other hand, is more personal. It is a quality of an individual to be honest and fair in his or her actions and words. This highlights that while ethics are more outwardly stated, integrity is something much more individualistic."*[1]

Yes, Eugene has a total lack of integrity. But, according to the National Retail Federation, it falls under the category of fraud, and losses from "return fraud" top $8.9 billion per year![2] They actually have a name for it — *Wardrobing!*

---

1   DifferenceBetween.com, "Difference Between Ethics and Integrity," January 13, 2015, Posted by Admin.

2   *Business Insider*, "Here's What Happens to a Product After You Return It to the Store," Kim Bhasin, January 2, 2013.

During the remainder of the week, Wardrobing Lucifer worked hard to keep his tags in his pants and sleeves, but it was known to one and all that Eugene was the "Minnie Pearl" of sales training.

Eugene was terminated shortly after he returned to his home office. It was not because of the "wardrobing" but because he wasn't working. I don't mean that he wasn't working out; I mean that he wasn't *working*. So, the company lost everything we invested in him from recruiting, to hiring, to onboarding and training, and of course, salary and car allowance.

➤❥ LUCIFER LESSON #1 ❧◀
Speak to the Issue

When an issue smacks you in the face, whether it's ethical, moral, criminal, or whatever, call it out.

When an issue smacks you in the face, whether it's ethical, moral, criminal, or whatever, call it out. Speak to it. Elevate awareness around it and above all, deliver feedback around it! Be direct, address the issue/behavior and not the person, set expectations, and gain agreement. Rinse and repeat.

➤❥ LUCIFER LESSON #2 ❧◀
The Value of Integrity

Integrity is easy to spot — Do what you say, be holistically honest, maintain your moral compass, and be respectful. Whenever you sense a slip in integrity, lead by example, set expectations, act with honesty and fairness, treat people with dignity and respect, and communicate!

Whenever you sense a slip in integrity, lead by example, set expectations, act with honesty and fairness, treat people with dignity and respect, and communicate!

I'll never forget the day that I returned from a local hotel where we held the five-day training session. I stepped off the elevator and ran smack dab into one of our executives. He asked where I was coming from. When I told him, he promptly barked; "Don't use that hotel anymore. We are going to cancel our contract with them on Monday!"

I didn't ask why, but the tone in his voice told me that he sure meant business. Unbeknownst to him, I had been invited to attend an NBA game that weekend with the director of sales for the very property that we were going to terminate our relationship with the following week. Ugh. I was looking forward to it so much. I had never been to an NBA game before, and these were really sweet seats. I felt deflated. It was late on Friday when I ran into the executive as he was heading out the door for the weekend. The game was for the very next evening, on Saturday. What am I going to do? I can't go to the game knowing that we are going to cancel our contract with them on Monday. I can't call her and tell her that we are cancelling our contract on Monday; it's not my place to do that. So, the next morning, I called the Director of Sales for the property and apologize up and down for my last-minute cancellation — a family emergency. Totally lame! But, she was very nice, and told me not to worry and expressed hope that everything worked out for me. Aside from the white lie — I held my head high. The value of integrity.

HIDDEN COSTS FROM WARDROBING LUCIFER

As innocuous as it seems, Wardrobing Lucifer had his own hidden costs and they all stem from integrity. Integrity is a quality. It speaks to one's ability to stand behind right versus wrong. We can ask ourselves, what was right with Wardrobing Lucifer? He seemed like a mild-mannered guy, but in reality he was a cheat. Knowingly and with intent, he cheated retailers out of their profit. That's a sure tell-tale sign of what he is capable of doing on the job, and how he lives his life. It sure panned out and came home to roost. He cheated the company in terms of work ethic. He skated, he ditched, he was not productive on the company clock. In fact, he used his time during the day to return clothes!

When Wardrobing Lucifer was terminated, we had to eat the recruiting and hiring costs. You know the drill, $1,875. We had to eat the training costs, which, by the way, included all of his onboarding (90 days long), salary, benefits and his trip to the corporate office for training; Cha-ching — $19,330. Not to mention the time and effort that an army of people put forth to make "the new hire" feel welcome and assimilated.

CHAPTER TEN

Curtain Call

This book shines a light on that certain type of salesperson that I call The Lucifer Leader who has the capability of derailing an organization by inciting other salespeople on the team to engage in illicit activity. They do so to acquire power and position amongst their peers, or to feed the underpinnings of their personality disorders. Thankfully, there aren't a lot of them out there, but there are enough to give the profession that "less than noble feeling."

LUCIFER REPRISE

You met **Charismatic Lucifer**, who is the poster child for the Lucifer Leader. His degree of influence is shocking. Identified by his lone wolf style, he has swagger and a silver tongue. He creates an air of interest fueled by his unorthodox tactics. It is his "don't play by the rules" approach that is most revealing. "Cavalier" screams lack of respect, and when you have lack of respect for process and the order of the organization, trouble usually follows.

Make sure that organizational fit is weighted higher than trait competitiveness during the recruitment and selection process. Take the time to share the meaningfulness of the work that they will be doing to influence organizational fit and reduce the potential for deviant behavior.

You met **Swindler Lucifer**, who is a con artist in disguise and a reminder to manage your hiring process effectively. The con artist is masterful at finding their marks. They use some serious skills to earn your confidence to gain access to your trust, your good will, and your compassion to carry out their fraudulent plans. If you have a lot of customer defection from a specific sales person, one who has a long history of job hopping, take a closer look; you might have a Swindler Lucifer on your hands!

You met **Criminal Lucifer**, who can potentially ruin your brand. By all accounts, he looks like a rising star, so the manager rushes him through the hiring process and neglects to complete the background check. You're doomed. Follow the hiring process. Don't skip mundane, but extremely important steps. Establish a "see something/say something" protocol at work, and make sure everyone is aware of it. Open a tip-line to help identify potential problems.

You met **Libertine Lucifer** and learned how their attention-seeking behavior can rob you blind. When a pre-hire assessment comes back positive, and yet, the presentation doesn't match the pre-conceived notion of what presents itself as "normal," that's a disconnect. A Red Flag! This Lucifer needs to be the center of attention and has a tendency to believe that relationships are more than they really are. They have low emotional intelligence and come across as overtly suggestive. Use good questioning skills during your interview to reconcile the disconnect.

You met **Monte Christo Lucifer** and saw how their wily ways can tank whole sales teams at one time. He is the consummate entertainer; the savior-faire, debonair who has power by virtue of the size of his wallet. Keep your eye on "the organizer": the guy or gal who emerges as a magnet. They draw people toward them and collect them like pawns. They could be legit leaders, or they could be a Lucifer.

You met **Voyeur Lucifer**, who offers a story beholden by competitiveness and the ultimate nightmare in the era of the #MeToo movement. Double-down on your own leadership skills and make the environment inclusive for everyone. When you see something that is off-color, somewhat indecent, or in poor taste, put a stop to it and investigate it. Nip it in the bud early before the virus spreads.

You met **Imperious Lucifer** and saw how the assumption of power and arrogance can cost you way more than you bargained for. A narcissistic leader, he has two sides. The first is fueled by his ego; it's the source of his energy. The second is his sociopathic underpinnings. The narcissist, in this case, fails to see his vulnerabilities and makes the environment uncomfortable. He lacks awareness of his destructive behavior even when direct feedback is delivered to him. The sociopath side of Imperious Lucifer possesses no empathy and gets bored easily if he is not constantly stirring the pot. Beware of the shiny object! When it sounds too good to be true, it probably is.

Don't be afraid to deliver frank feedback to a Lucifer like this and engage in good performance management practices no matter what level the person holds in the organization. Stage an intervention if you must. The earlier you get it out on the table the better. Establish expectations, align goals, and provide feedback. Revisit this often. If things are not moving in the right direction, take action before it's too late.

Finally, you met **Wardrobing Lucifer**. When an issue smacks you in the face (whether it's ethical, moral, criminal, or whatever), call it out. Speak to it. Elevate awareness around it and above all, deliver feedback around it! Be direct, address the issue not the person, set expectations, and gain agreement. Rinse and repeat.

THE VALUE OF POSSIBILITIES

Now, let's imagine that our cast of characters walked back out on the stage for their final bow (after all, this chapter is titled "Curtain Call"). What might be the possibilities if this cast was made up of great sales people with excellent organizational citizenship? The value could total $17,018,877! This is the sum total of what just eight of our Lucifer Leaders have cost their organizations!

Ask yourself: *Could you be sacrificing cultural fit and adaptive behaviors in an effort to fill open positions?*

KEEP IN TOUCH!

What brings great sales people to your organization? What Lucifer Leader stories do you have to share? Visit my website to continue the conversation and get free tools on how to help you deal with the Lucifers that walk among you! www.luciferleaders.com

Send me an email at:

✉ kkoultourides@kknowhow.com

Follow me on social media:

🔗 www.linkedin.com/in/kathy-koultourides-salesexpert
🐦 Twitter.com/KathyKoultourides

GO BEYOND THE BOOK

Hire Kathy to:

- Build a solid sales onboarding program to get your new hires off on the right foot.

- Create a customized sales training program that inspires top skills.

- Conduct workshops on selling skills, negotiation skills, people skills, interviewing, coaching and delivering feedback.

- Design and develop custom e-Learning courses.

- Deliver key-note break-out sessions at sales meetings.

ACKNOWLEDGEMENTS

I would never have thought that writing a book would be challenging. Writing has always come easy to me, ever since I could hold a pencil. I was a finalist, in the fifth grade, for the Chicagoland Area Father of The Year award with my essay on "Why My Father Should Be Father of The Year." I am a consummate letter writer and card sender. My husband is always in awe at the speed and eloquence I lay down on a difficult sympathy card. But, writing a book, wow! It had its ups and downs. The stories were easy; I'm a good storyteller but pulling it all together took me some time. I had a very bad case of "*The Bitch*" whispering in my head that the book is not good, or it's too silly. It was with the support of so many people that I triumphed to deliver this work to my readers. And, I owe many thanks to so many people that helped me on my journey:

First, to my writing coach, **Cathy Fyock**, for all her support, wisdom, coaching and leadership. I am so grateful for your patience and guidance. You are a master at business book writing, and a kind and generous person! I'm proud to call you my friend.

Next, a huge thank you to my editorial review board. Your feedback helped me put the finishing touches on this book and helped me beef it up by almost 4,000 words! Many thanks to **Andy Martin, Cathy Berlin, Cathy Fyock, Jim Holton, Karen Connolly** and **Tony Petrucci**. I appreciate the time you took to read my manuscript and provide me with your unique business perspectives, especially in light of the fact that you all have full-time, demanding jobs. You are all wonderful!

Thank you to **my many friends and colleagues** who read portions of my book and offered endorsements and words of encouragement. Your support is appreciated and inspiring.

To my publisher, **Kate Colbert**, thank you for putting your faith in me! It is with great honor that my book is among the titles of your wonderful company. Thank you for the care and attention you provided to me throughout the publishing journey. Your team at Silver Tree Publishing is top notch!

To my husband **George**, for patiently dealing with my roller-coaster writing process and cooking a lot of dinners while I pecked away at the keyboard.

To **my mom and dad, Bob and Norma Kaplan**. Thank you for listening to me talk endlessly about my book (for two years), even when it was a pipe dream. Your love and support are truly special. And, thank you for nurturing my sense of humor; if anything, this book is funny! Thanks to my sisters, Linda and Debbie and my brother Mark for buying hundreds of copies to give as gifts to your friends! XOXO!

To my life-long friend and business partner, **Dave Neuweiler**, who read the first story I composed, way back in 2016, and sits with bated-breath to be the very first person to buy the very first copy on Amazon.com!

And finally, to all my friends, old and new, who celebrate this special accomplishment with me! You are the BEST!!!!

ABOUT THE AUTHOR

Kathy Koultourides, CPLP® is a nationally
acclaimed award-winning Sales Trainer
and ATD Certified Professional in Learning
and Performance, who utilizes her strong
business background and learning and
organizational development expertise to
guide businesses on how to best improve
results through customized learning and
talent development strategies.

Kathy is an accomplished public speaker
and is featured in 52 videos for Cornell University's Prendismo
Collection, spanning topics on Negotiation, Sales, Leadership and
Gender Issues in business. She is a skillful facilitator who uses
a wide-range of techniques in the areas of sales training, call center
skills, interviewing, communication skills, change management,
coaching & leadership, and team building. She is an expert in the
design and development of new hire onboarding using a blended
approach for maximum return on investment.

Kathy believes in a holistic approach to learning and development
and follows the Six Disciplines of Breakthrough Learning® whereby
she begins with defining the business outcome, designing a complete

experience, delivers for application, drives learning transfer, deploys performance support and documents results.[1]

Kathy lives with her husband in Fountain Hills, Arizona. *Lucifer Leaders* is her first nonfiction business book.

---

1   The 6D's Company, Andy Jefferson, Co-founder CEO and Roy Pollock, Founder and Chief Learning Officer.

Made in the USA
Middletown, DE
29 October 2018